A Heart Set on Pilgrimage
The LifeLine Way

A Heart Set on Pilgrimage
The LifeLine Way

John Singleton
with Daniel Singleton

Copyright © 2017 John Singleton and Daniel Singleton.

All rights reserved. No part of this work may be reproduced or transmitted in any for or by any means, electronic or mechanical, including photocopying, recording or by any information storage and retrieval system without permission in writing from the publisher, except where allowed by law.

Cover illustration © 2017 Tanya Farrugia.
Cover design © 2017 LifeLine Design.

Scripture quotations taken from the HOLY BIBLE, NEW INTERNATIONAL VERSION. Copyright © 1973, 1978, 1984 by International Bible Society. Used by permission of Hodder & Stoughton, a member of the Hodder Headline Group. All rights reserved. 'NIV' is a trademark of International Bible Society. UK trademark number 1448790.

Scripture taken from The Message. Copyright © 1993, 1994, 1995, 1996, 2000, 2001, 2002. Used by permission of NavPress Publishing Group.

Scripture texts in this work are taken from the New American Bible, revised edition © 2010, 1991, 1986, 1970 Confraternity of Christian Doctrine, Washington, D.C. and are used by permission of the copyright owner. All Rights Reserved. No part of the New American Bible may be reproduced in any form without permission in writing from the copyright owner.

Scripture taken from the NEW AMERICAN STANDARD BIBLE®, Copyright © 1960, 1962, 1963, 1968, 1971, 1972, 1973, 1975, 1977, 1995 by The Lockman Foundation. Used by permission.

The Holy Bible: International Standard Version. Release 2.0, Build 2015.02.09. Copyright © 1995–2014 by ISV Foundation. ALL RIGHTS RESERVED INTERNATIONALLY. Used by permission of Davidson Press, LLC.

Holy Bible, New Living Translation, copyright © 1996, 2004, 2015 by Tyndale House Foundation. Used by permission of Tyndale House Publishers Inc., Carol Stream, Illinois 60188. All rights reserved.

From the Good News Bible published by the Bible Societies and HarperCollins Publishers, © American Bible Society 1994, used with permission.

ISBN 978-0-244-32204-5

First printed 2017.
Printed and bound by Lulu.

"Politics which works depends on long established values being widely shared. Some people are surprised to discover that, in today's secular Britain, those values are being most effectively renewed in churches and faith groups. Our All-Party Parliamentary Group is committed to supporting them. LifeLine, under John Singleton's leadership, has an outstanding record of effective witness, and of pioneering imaginative local solutions, for as long as I have known them. I commend this warm and lively account of the LifeLine story."

— Rt Hon Stephen Timms, MP for East Ham
Chair, All-Party Parliamentary Group on Faith and Society

"In *A Heart Set on Pilgrimage*, my friend Daniel Singleton and his father John, share personal stories with real value for the church. There are lessons to be drawn on here for all church leaders and followers of Jesus that will enliven our communities and strengthen our faith for the years ahead. I am so grateful for them sharing these experiences and great learnings for us in this gift of a book."

— Michael Wear, author
Reclaiming Hope: Lessons Learned in the Obama White House About the Future of Faith in America

"Be prepared for a rollercoaster ride with the spiritual 'Godfather' of East London that will challenge you to the core! John and his family, along with the LifeLine Church, are probably one of the UK's best kept secrets with a remarkable story to tell. And here it is! Inspirational, packed with kingdom conviction and hilariously real; we need like never before to be reminded of our history, of why authentic church still counts and why we do what we do. We have been inspired and challenged by John's life, community, generosity and teaching and now we get to have the full story that offers honesty, wisdom and direction for our own lives and leadership adventures still to be lived!"

— TIM AND ANIA ANDERSON, PLUMBLINE GB

"As a couple who have just planted a church into Belfast, it is so refreshing to hear John and Daniel's heart for the church to reclaim its adventurous, bold, expectant and 'all-in' heritage. As we start out on our church-planting adventure, it is invaluable to have the wisdom of others to draw on. Using biblical examples, personal stories and practical insight from the journey of LifeLine, this book holds out the standard of New Testament church living and inspires the Church to really love one another and to recommit to Jesus' call to reach and help the poor, the sick, the outcast and the refugee. A really helpful and challenging read."

— DAVID AND JOY DICKINSON, LEADERS, CARNMONEY CENTRAL

"John and Daniel have unveiled a timely contribution to a better tomorrow. This is not just a book, it is a true story and a template of valuable treasures from of the heart for people on life's journey who want to arrive at the right destination.

This work is unique because it really does speak as you read. I could hear John's voice since I have had great opportunities to hear him speak on a number of the subjects addressed in this book in home setting, at conferences and even fun times. If you know John, you must agree with me that he lives what he's put down in writing.

This book cuts across generations and it is no wonder a father and son put it together. The LifeLine Way is clearly mapped, the destination is certain. I believe Daniel's love for history contributed to the in-depth presentations of facts, dates and places as seen in this book. I think I now know the man who will chronicle The LifeLine Way for generations to come.

Thanks John and Daniel for this book. We can now eat the meat and spit the bones and if needs be we shall bury the car."

— Dr. Albert S. L. Kitcher, President, Today's Family
Ghanaian Honorary Consul to Ukraine

"This book is helpful to individuals who want to go forward with God in a relationship that is real, trustworthy, passionate and zealous.

Many times we try to serve God without reflecting on our journey and the pathway we have walked. But it's always a requirement from God that we re-examine our ways.

John is a living testimony of living a life that is set on pilgrimage. He has modelled the Christ life before us not just in words but by example.

He does not just preach sermons but is walking the message of Christ that he communicates. Relationship is not just a topic for us but real life experience, shared and felt together. John is very interested in the person, the individual, family, children, leaders, the church and the unchurched.

Our welfare and relevance is more important to him than wanting to come to preach in the church or meetings. All he wanted was to come spend time with us, interact with us, share a meal with us, interactive in our concerns and know about us face to face.

For us it has been 30 years of real life experiences one after the other with John and LifeLine. The expression of pilgrimage is real life values demonstrated by a man with his friends. John does not only talk the talk, but walk the walk. Indeed he is a "hearer and a doer of the word".

The principles addressed in this book are treasures we have used to communicate with our people in the Caribbean, Africa, Asia and the US. We re-evaluate these to strengthen our relationship with God and each other. To ensure that we are not running on our own strength but connecting with the Holy Spirit as He leads us through the path of God's Kingdom advance."

— HILTON ALBERT, LIFELINE CARIBBEAN COORDINATOR, SAINT MARTIN

"There is so much to appreciate and admire about the father and son duo of John Singleton and Daniel Singleton. One of the things that I love the most is their pursuit of and commitment to real relationships which I am so pleased they have written about because there is much we can all learn from them. This book is packed with stories from forty years of church ministry and the lessons for those who want to learn from these experiences. This is an account of how LifeLine has gone from being a collection of home groups, to affecting their local community through social action and social enterprise and working in partnership overseas, to see other communities changed as well, always with relationship at the core."

— Matt Bird, Founder, the Cinnamon Network

"The heart set on pilgrimage is intent on a better world. A sure sign that God is at work is when people find themselves doing things they never dreamt possible, or likely (burying cars?), acting as leaven for the world God holds precious (Matt. 13:33). This book tells of such pilgrimage.

That 'the love of Christ compels us' (2 Cor. 5:14) to social action as well as worshipping community shines through this story. It acclaims the Holy Spirit, moving and invigorating where He wills, not where we will; working with our foibles and failings as much as our strengths and successes.

This book confronts, inspires and amuses. People of all Christian traditions will recognise and value much here. The great mystic Meister Eckhart told us that the God who takes covenant with us so seriously also delights and laughs with and at us, and if we let down our defences woos us into doing the same. That God delights, laughs and dances through these pages, the people in them, and the people they serve. This book tells a story of God and His people hopelessly in love, and that love spilling out to build a better world."

— Prof. Jim McManus, OCDS, CPsychol, CSci, AFBPsS, FFPH, FCIEH, FRSB
Director of Public Health, Hertfordshire County Council
Hon. Professor, Schools of Health and Social Work and Life and Medical Sciences, University of Hertfordshire

In dedicating this book, I want to borrow a phrase from Hebrews 12:1 and recognise the 'great cloud of witnesses' past, present and future.

With particular thanks to my wife Dawn and my family.

But of course this is a story about our special community at LifeLine Church and LifeLine Network – we are journeying together.

...and now to the next adventure!

Contents

Acknowledgements	XIII
Foreword	XV

Introduction
A note on translations, glossary, and approach to storytelling	3
The monument stones	13

I. Caught, not Taught – The Foundations
A hint of what was to come	21
Eat the meat, spit out the bones	27
Old Thompson	37
As I stood with piles of clothes at my feet…	43

II. Discovering on the Job
God wears out carpets	53
So we buried the car	61
Meals and Mars Bars	65

III. Drinking at Many Streams
The lesson of Bob	71
A different way to build	77
Kingdom without borders	83
Apostolic community	95
Hearing it, saying it, doing it – integrity and faith	101
The chapter we didn't want to write – Splits, division, leaving and soft-heartedness	107
The Spirit of Adventure	113

Acknowledgements

Many people have been involved in bringing this book together. The book contains stories of people, not all of whom are still with us, but for whom we are immensely grateful. Everyone has been wonderfully generous in giving their time and effort, without you all we wouldn't have been able to fulfil God's word to us to 'write our story.'

Over an extended period, I had received a number of these 'nudges' from God to write a book. Eventually it became quite pressing. After a couple of abortive attempts, one day Daniel said, "Let's face it – you're unlikely to give the time to do this. You talk, and I will write". Significantly, Daniel's ability to write was being increasingly recognised. He was able to capture the direction of my thoughts as well as the heart attitude, making for an accurate representation, and I am very grateful for the end product – which is the result not only of his writing gift but of his diligence, forward thinking and committed determination to the purpose.

Special mention has to go to my family: Dawn and my sons – Daniel, Nathan and Jamie – who crop up at various points in the book, sometimes explicitly and sometimes anonymously to protect the guilty!

Particular thanks go to our immediate team: Rodie Garland for her uncompromising editorial skills, Margaret Akerman for her eagle-eyed proofing; Lisa Webb, Avril McIntyre, Anthony McKernan, Heidi Singleton, Felicity Smith, Rebecca Coles, Sally Dixon and Judi Singleton for their hands-on support during writing; Elspeth Paisley for managing the book production process along with Chris Miller, typesetter extraordinaire; Tanya Farrugia for giving her illustrative talents to produce a beautiful cover; the whole of the FaithAction team for acting as sounding boards; Hugh Osgood and all those who took time to read the manuscript and give such generous feedback; the launch team who helped to shape the book in its initial stages. Last, but not least we want to thank those who have walked with us and been part of the stories we tell in the book.

Foreword

A Heart Set on Pilgrimage is an amazing book. I love the way in which John Singleton has so freely shared his thoughts, feelings and experiences, and I can see that Daniel, as co-writer, has done the same. Few people would share in such an open and relational way, clearly motivated by an overwhelming desire to serve those of us who are keen to learn from the LifeLine journey.

It has been my privilege to travel alongside LifeLine at different times on this journey and there are some things that stand out about LifeLine Church and the LifeLine network that should have us all scurrying to this book for a privileged look at their inner workings.

The first thing is the transparency. Here we have a church and a network where the members of the leadership team will always speak plainly about their challenges and aspirations. Secondly, we find in every area of LifeLine a willingness to constantly review and learn from others. Thirdly, there are very few organisations that I have come across around the world that come anywhere close to LifeLine's effectiveness in the whole area of implementation. LifeLine will never let the grass grow under its feet. If there is something that God is challenging LifeLine to do, implementation strategies will be underway while others waste time thinking of excuses.

These three reasons alone should be sufficient incentive to draw on the lessons laid out for us in the stories in this book, but if I were to go for a fourth, it would be inspiration. I can honestly say that LifeLine Church and Network constantly inspire and now, through this book, you can be inspired too.

— Hugh Osgood
President, Churches in Communities International

Introduction

A note on translations, glossary, and approach to storytelling

Our base Bible translation tends to be the New International Version (NIV), but I grew up with people reading from the King James Version (KJV) or, as it was often called, the Authorised Version (AV). As such, the way I recall verses is something of a mish-mash between versions – which creates a bit of a nightmare when I am searching for a particular verse. What we have sought to do here is to use the version that comes closest to showing the significance to us of the verse in question. The NIV is very sound, but it is not as memorable as other versions. Unless otherwise noted, scripture quotations will be from the NIV; the other main Bible versions used here are:

The Message (MSG)
The New America Bible (NAB)
The New American Standard Version (NASB)
The International Standard Version (ISV)
New Living Translation (NLT)
Good News (GNT)

STORYTELLING

Jesus gave us a great example in his teaching by using parables; we also know that one of the most powerful ways of communicating is through personal testimony. We have sought to combine the two here. We are not so creative as to make up our own pictorial parables, but have instead used real stories. At least, the roots of these stories are real. There will be issues of accuracy in the detail: some have of course been simplified, and some will be told the way I remember them – this book does span 40 years, after all. Thus the stories are meant more as parables than as an historically accurate account. So if we have got things wrong, we are not seeking to make an excuse – merely to tell a greater story of God working with us and the lessons we have picked up along the way. If you have been giving sermons as long as I have, and have listened to people feed back what they have taken away from your talk, you will no doubt wonder if they were in the same talk as the one you gave! Well, as Paul says:

> *But what does it matter? The important thing is that in every way, whether from false motives or true, Christ is preached. And because of this I rejoice. Yes, and I will continue to rejoice...*
> — **Phil. 1:18**

A Glossary of Terminology

The house church movement

I hope that we express ourselves clearly here, but I think it is worth just giving a little explanation of what I mean by 'house church'. This refers to the church movement in the late 1960s onwards which was characterised by people leaving or being asked to leave traditional church denominations and beginning to meet in homes. The catalyst was a growing desire for the 'restoration' of church life akin to what we read of in the New Testament. This was related to the everyday expectation of the supernatural and spiritual gifts in our lives, but also to God-enabled relationships.

I had seen the supernatural as a Pentecostal, but the meetings' focus and lack of real relationship left unmet the desire that God had set in me. I wanted to explore the practice of New Testament church rather than just the theory. So the early years of LifeLine became a quest to rediscover the community of relationship that God first intended for us.

The house church movement comes under many titles: restoration, new church, etc., but at its root there are some differences from evangelical charismatic churches, particularly with regard to the focus on depth of relationship. This is not to command some idea of exclusivity, but rather to try to help you see the radical simple desire for relationship and fullness of life in Christ Jesus.

Apostolic community and apostolic ministry

An apostolic community is a community of people who are 'receiving an apostle in the name of an apostle' and thereby gaining that particular benefit (see Matt. 10:41). This is best explained with reference to Ephesians 4, as God's method of transferring a tiny proportion of His apostolic anointing to His church to equip them in the ways that He wants them equipped. It means that the apostle (person) has to be received, and recognised as carrying that anointing, but not worshipped or held on a pedestal. At the end of the day they are simply a transportation system.

The characteristics or features of an apostolic community would include the following:

A sending or giving mentality arising from an ability to look beyond their own community. The 'worldview' is not that everybody from the community travels, but that resources will be released from among them for God's wider world. The apostolic anointing is not for the apostle alone but 'trickles down' so that the community is characterised by creativity, breakthrough and the birthing of new expressions of the Kingdom of God.

Never being content simply to hear, but expecting to see the things in action that God is saying and doing (Ps. 48:8).

Having attitudes and actions regarding issues like money, integrity, relationship, righteousness and serving that reflect biblical principles rather than limited church traditions. You would certainly expect that people would say what they mean and mean what they say. You would expect real relationships expressed in caring and sharing and giving, and where truth can be spoken in love. Decision making is based on righteousness and principle, not convenience and pragmatism. Serving happens where there is need rather than in the pursuit of ministry or preference. As a group they are focused far beyond simply being small or introspective 'care units', and meetings in a building are just a small part of their life.

You would expect the community to 'produce' more than it 'consumes', so that it might release resources for God's purposes in the earth. That would include a commitment to training and equipping, not simply maintaining the community's existence.

An attitude inclined towards innovation, and a readiness to go wherever God is saying in terms of developing new approaches (Matt. 13:52). To that end, there would be a willingness to draw from a variety of sources, and not being limited to 'drinking at one stream'.

LifeLine Church

LifeLine Church was birthed in north east London over three decades ago. With its roots in the house church movement of the 1970s, the focus is on demonstrating the love of God to the people and communities it is involved with.

The church has always prioritised people over property and so tends to think of itself as 'not so much a building, more a way of life'.

Living in good relationship with God and one another is a foundational practice of the church. High priority is placed on sharing life together and following Jesus.

The church is very purposeful, expecting to hear God and live by His Spirit daily. The church also has a generous posture which has resulted in significant investment in people, projects and places over the years – both locally and overseas.

In addition to the usual activities that build the faith of individuals – teaching, prayer, worship, small groups, youth groups and children's work – there is also a pioneering and creative edge that engages with people in a relevant way and stays clear of the restrictions of traditions.

LifeLine Projects

LifeLine Church has always been active in the community, and in 2000 a sister charity, LifeLine Projects, was established to support a fresh set of social action projects in east London.

Following an investment of £20,000 from the church, the charity grew to an annual income of over £5 million, with significant public funding.

It has enabled LifeLine to affect more people and deliver greater impact in local communities.

Projects have included running Children's Centres, helping people to find work, delivering parenting classes, supporting new mums and teaching money management. More recent projects include mentoring vulnerable young people, running an independent alternative school, working with ex-offenders and establishing a chain of nurseries.

There are strong partnerships with local schools, local government, central government, health care professionals and related agencies.

FaithAction

The experience and track record of LifeLine Projects' work in east London enabled a network of faith-based and community organisations to be developed.

Originally funded by the Cabinet Office before becoming a member of the Department of Health's Voluntary Sector Strategic Partnership (now the Health and Wellbeing Alliance), FaithAction has over 2,000 members nationally and works with over 70 partners across government and the voluntary and faith sectors.

FaithAction funds, trains, advises, researches, and innovates to support local faith-based organisations at work in their communities. In partnership with Queen Mary University of London, it developed and now runs the Creative English programme. First birthed by Dr Anne Smith, a member of Lifeline Church, Creative English is one of the community-based English language programmes funded by the Department for Communities & Local Government and available by licence to community groups throughout the UK. FaithAction also acts as the secretariat for the All-Party Parliamentary Group on Faith and Society.

In recent times, work has been undertaken at the intersection of faith and public health. FaithAction has researched, written on and trained others in areas including alcohol abuse, housing and homelessness and domestic violence. It also runs Friendly Places, a campaign to ensure faith organisations are welcoming and safe places for those with mental health struggles.

LifeLine Network International

We have formed friendships and connections with church leaders and others around the world over more than 25 years. These friendships have birthed an international network of partners who support each other across ministries with regular visits, conferences and training opportunities. These are genuine two-way relationships with much learning flowing each way.

LifeLine Network is very purposeful, fighting poverty and injustice and seeking to make practical differences in local communities. Farming, micro-finance, counselling, vocational training and education are just some of the many projects currently undertaken by our partners in 17 countries.

Community Resources

Community Resources grows creative solutions to local issues – solutions provided by the community, for the community. Powered by volunteers from all walks of life, the team brings people together to realise that they can make a great contribution to their community.

Among the solutions are a number of 'Connecting Places': environments where people can start friendships, develop skills and confidence and discover what they can contribute. This isn't about having a venue, doing a project or running a service – although all of these things happen. It is about inviting local people to get involved and try out new ideas that benefit the locality.

Our Connecting Places include the Community Hub, the Corner Coffee House and personal development groups that explore different subjects, helping people to make positive life choices.

Peaced Together

Peaced Together was developed in 2012 by my son Daniel's wife, Heidi Singleton, then a teacher in east London. After a difficult time in her life, she found hope and restoration through the creative process and started writing Peaced Together.

Using a variety of themed craft projects, Peaced Together encourages participants to reflect on their lives and set out on a personal journey from brokenness to hope. The course consists of five craft projects. Each one helps participants to explore topics such as beauty, thankfulness and positive choices.

Peaced Together is suitable for women of any age, and it particularly benefits women who feel isolated or depressed, or are victims of abuse. The course has helped 500 women so far and has been run across the UK and internationally.

DOULOS

Doulos is a nine-month development course that we first started running in the late 1980s. There are three key elements: teaching, a mentor or personal trainer and a project. This programme has proved to be a crucible of personal development for those who have taken part, as they journey together with other Doulos team members. Doulos is highly sought-after among LifeLine Network International members, with programmes taking place in the Caribbean, western and southern Africa as well as in the United Kingdom. The name *'Doulos'* is from ancient Greek and is the term for the most humble servant or slave.

Are we in danger of a lack of thankfulness — of forgetting, or retreating from, the high ground that we took with pain and sacrifice?

Thankfulness is a choice.

The monument stones

As a group of people, we have always been very much against tradition for tradition's sake, and certainly very much against legalism. However, we now find ourselves very much for monument, testimony and thanksgiving. The key difference between the former and latter is a grappling with purpose.

Why:

>   are we doing this?

>   are we saying that?

>   are we where we are?

If we fall into a lifeless, nostalgic recounting of the past, we are indulging in something 'soulish' and our narrative, rather than leading to new heights, leads to a cul-de-sac. However, if we lack the ability to recount what God has done, and what we have learned from those experiences for our faith today, we have failed to tap into a living testimony of God's provision. The horizon of our faith is limited by our lack of history.

My boys would sit and listen to the stories my father told of growing up between the wars and fighting in the Second World War as a firefighter during the Blitz and on D-Day. Daniel attributes his love of history and his becoming a history teacher to learning to appreciate the stories of the past from my dad, and to learning about the battles that those who came before us fought for the freedoms we enjoy today.

It is interesting that my father could always see the hand of God in his most extreme experiences, to the point that he felt that the life-changing injury he received in Normandy was part of God's plan for his life. Spotting the hand of God over a period of time is something that can only be done on reflection. It helps us get a sense of His graceful eternal nature and our limited finite one.

This reflecting on what has happened in the past, the journey that has been taken and the lessons that we are meant to learn is a key part of shaping our identity. There is a lack of generational storytelling, and this is akin to making barren an older generation and orphans of the next generation. In this way – if we are no different from the world – the church merely reflects the world rather than shining a light on an alternative way of being.

As Joshua approaches the river Jordan in Joshua chapter 3, two significant things are noted. There is a miraculous intervention by God as '… all Israel crossed on dry ground…' (Josh. 3:17, NAB; emphasis added). The crossing of the Jordan is significant for all kinds of reasons. As we as Christians move to greater maturity, we see a helpful pattern in the story of Joshua, which takes the children of Israel from an immature, hand-to-mouth existence, totally reliant on God, to a new position where they must cultivate the earth and take part in warfare alongside God as they take possession of the Promised Land.

I believe this is a picture for today. We are co-heirs with Christ: we have good works to do as well as spiritual interactions. Note it was all of the nation of Israel who crossed over, and again, the author emphasises: 'After the entire nation had crossed the Jordan…' (Josh. 4:1, NAB; emphasis added). No one is left behind, no one has their own separate story at this point. The whole nation crosses to take possession of the promise.

The second significant point is that all twelve tribes put down monument stones: they were all part of the victory and the promise! Yet in Joshua 22, several of the tribes were released to go back across the Jordan to the land to the east that they had been allotted. They crossed with the whole nation[1], and then once the land was subdued for their brothers, they returned to the Jordan for what was theirs. So, we learn from this that there is an importance in all taking hold of the promise:

---

1   Earlier in the story Joshua tells the tribes to leave the women and children in the camp, but the emphasis is on the whole nation – there is a sense of togetherness.

we don't just do it for ourselves – the collective is important, and we all share in the victory. There were twelve stones, not ten. The monument could be viewed and owned from both sides of the Jordan.

It would also seem that there was not just one monument of twelve stones, but several. One stood in the river itself (Josh. 4:9) to mark the place where the priest had stood when the waters were stopped, and another was placed at Gilgal (Josh. 4:20) as a testimony to the children – for those who would 'come after'. There is no way around it: we need to note, share and give thanks for God's work in our lives and in the lives of those who have gone before us!

The Old Testament is a constant, repeating story of forgetting. God designs a good path for His people, they stray from His plans and purpose and suffer because of this, and then He brings rescue. The pattern is repeated again and again – familiarity breeds contempt, the young don't learn the lessons of the old and the old are unable to convey those messages: experience is not the instructor it should be. This forgetting demonstrates a lack of thankfulness for what God has done – a loss of understanding of the abhorrence of sin and a lack of passion for righteousness.

So, as we enter the 21st century, how does this fit with us?

Are we in danger of a lack of thankfulness – of forgetting, or retreating from, the high ground that we took with pain and sacrifice?

Older generations often say the young have it too easy. However, the real issue is a lack of appreciation: after all, what parent or grandparent does not want improvements in the lives of their offspring?

A number of years ago, while in conversation with my builder, as I started to go downstairs, I missed a step with one foot, lost my balance, spun on the other leg, causing a complete rupture of the quadratic tendons and would have sailed down the stairs head first if it wasn't for the builder and Daniel grabbing me as I started to fall. It was a very real brush with my own mortality, which gave me a new perspective on life. What followed was a number of months of intense physio and a major operation on my leg. In one step I had lost my independence and my ability to walk unaided. Boy, did I learn to appreciate walking – and I was determined to get my abilities back. I couldn't take it for granted: I had to go into intense training to be able to walk again. By

God's grace – at least I choose to believe it was grace – we had just started as a church going through the book of James. Suddenly James 1:2–4 had a new bite:

> *Consider it pure joy, my brothers and sisters, whenever you face trials of many kinds, because you know that the testing of your faith produces perseverance. Let perseverance finish its work so that you may be mature and complete, not lacking anything.*
>
> — JAMES 1:2–4

I was all for agreeing with Martin Luther, at this point, who is reputed to have thought that maybe we could leave James out of the Bible altogether. Nevertheless, there it was in black and white: 'Consider it pure joy' (or, as is written in 1 Thess. 5, 'in all circumstances give thanks'!) Choosing to be thankful is not an impulsive feeling: it is a choice. In fact, much of the great action of Christian life cannot be left to feelings: the same goes for love, forgiveness, commitment and so on. Building a monument of thankfulness is a deliberate exercise. We learned so much through this period of time: as my wife Dawn put it, "God wasn't surprised… John's fall was a surprise to us but not to Him"

So we are choosing to be thankful and to recount the activity of our Lord in our lives.

It is interesting that in many cultures there is an oral tradition of reciting the history of the nation or tribe, to bring full context to the present day in a time of decision-making and planning. Recounting in this way is not nostalgic, but strategic.

Our cup of narrative has to be running over the edges with the 'why' of our story; with aims and purpose. As we tell of what happened in the past, this cannot be a fuzzy, rose-tinted remembering; it has to articulate the purposes and presence of God in our lives.

If this book represents nothing other than an account of thankfulness, it will have done a good thing. However, testimony leads to cries of 'Amen', 'Do it again, Lord!'[2] It heightens our expectation and takes us on a wonderful, hopeful thought-journey of 'What if…?'

We felt God prompt us to 'write things down' a number of times. This book, then, is a response to that, and maybe even an act of repentance: it has taken us some time to do it.

So the purpose of this book is to tell our story, in a way which can be of use to those who want to learn from our journey, and to raise up a monument to what God has done. It should show the essential seeds sown in my life and that of the church — which have affected the way we have built and grown.

Like the monument at the Jordan, this is not a 'looking back' monument, but a standard raised up to speak to our future — while recognising the journey that we are on or, as we often say, the 'pilgrimage'.

---

2 There is no doubt that testimony releases faith in the hearers. Some scholars say that testimony has a prophetic edge: it releases a 'do it again, Lord' anointing (Rev. 19:10).

I
CAUGHT, NOT TAUGHT
The Foundations

I started to learn that walking together on our journey of faith could be enjoyed, not just endured.

Church life is so much more than meetings. Relationship is at the core of who God made us to be, so it's through relationship with each other, in our homes, that we find welcome and rest, a place to gather and a place to grow.

A hint of what was to come

It's so easy to adopt a disposable approach to life. We don't repair things any more – we throw away and replace. If something no longer works the way we want it to, we throw it out and it's almost as if it was never there. Although much of what we say is about 'moving on', we must not lose sight of the 'great cloud of witnesses' (Heb. 12:1) who came before us. It is the hard graft of their faith that we stand on, their hard fought battles which we live the other side of. I never want to be disrespectful of those who have been true to the revelation and understanding that they had. I have less sympathy for, or comprehension of, those who have abstained from obtaining high heights and settled for something less. In that sense, I have no time for tradition: doing something again and again just because 'that is what we have always done' seems pointless to me. We are called not to waste time: 'Be very careful, then, how you live – not as unwise but as wise, making the most of every opportunity, because the days are evil.' (Eph. 5:15–16). I don't believe the Bible gives us much room for drift.

In my early faith there were three families who opened the doors of their homes and had a profound impact on me, often around the edges of what they thought they were bringing to me. It was the atmosphere of these homes that had the impact. At this time, I was part of a vibrant Pentecostal church in Dagenham, east London. I had grown up in a small Pentecostal church in Hertfordshire and had drifted from the faith of my parents, but God drew me back to Himself and I was not prepared to settle for the limited expression, a 'half-life' of faith that I felt characterised my home church. I had started a journey that would result in my becoming a church planter, but it was a gradual journey, in which I didn't know that the destination that God had planned for me was much greater and beyond my furthest imaginings and understanding. Nonetheless, when I came back to God my heart was 'set on pilgrimage' (Ps. 84:5), and I wasn't going to settle for something less than what God had for me.

What I saw in these homes was something like when you are in a dark room and the door opens just a crack into another room where the light is on. The edges of the door are framed with light and you realise there is the possibility of something else: the reality you are in is not the only thing on the menu.

We knew that our faith was expressed not only on a Sunday morning, and that it should affect our lives for the rest of the week as well. However, church life was pretty much limited to meetings. So in not restricting our faith to a Sunday morning, the answer was to have more meetings. Sunday was wiped out with meetings – morning, afternoon and evening with some additional prayer groups and study times – as well as various midweek combinations. So it was almost by accident that I started to see the home, the family and relationship as core to Christian life and church.

Each of these homes reflected the 'flavour' of the householder, and each was an open door into the idea of relationship – outside of meetings! I started to learn that walking together on our journey of faith could be enjoyed, not just endured.

Isn't it interesting that of the many times Jesus says that we should 'do' something to one another (love, forgive etc.), only handful of these instructions could be carried out in the setting of a corporate meeting or church service. The great majority need a relational setting or a place of fellowship to achieve God's practical commands.

Houses which made a difference

I was travelling between work in the City of London, my parents' home in Hertfordshire and the church in Dagenham. One family in Becontree, Dagenham, let me stay on their couch whenever I needed to. They were always so welcoming whenever I came by, interested in me and encouraging. It makes a big difference when, although you know you are imposing on someone, you are made to feel that they are pleased you came. They provided more than a place to sleep: it was a place to rest as well. A *place of welcome* – it was filed in the back of my mind.

The next place I remember was in Rush Green, near Romford. This was a *place to gather*. As the general understanding at the time was that church life meant meetings, there was not much in the way of additional socialising – you saw people at meetings and then you went on your way. Rush Green was different. There was always a crowd of young people just hanging out, having a laugh and enjoying being together. This home was a gathering home, somewhere for people to go. It was friendly – you didn't need to be lonely. I have often heard people say, 'When I have a house in the right area I'll be happy, and I'll have people round', or 'When I'm married', or 'When I have kids'. The point is that there is always a reason not to do something. Hospitality is a state of heart, not a location issue. This home was a bit out of the way, but everyone gathered there still, because they wanted to be there.

Finally, there was the home of Len and Elsie Halls. They were later to become my in-laws – but that was some way off. Their home in Ingleby Road was a *place to grow*. At Ingleby Road there was always discussion, and even at times arguments, but people rarely fell out. It was a novel thing to see fervent interactions and even passionate debates, and yet have these not damage relationships but strengthen them. There was instruction, but this was always connected to lifestyle: how were we to live? How did the teaching affect how we were, day to day? Discussion exposed what you didn't know, but that was good because we would wrestle out the answers. This was about progression and development; it wasn't a cosy huddle. Len had great little phrases and his own unique way of quoting the Bible. He would often say, 'I believe in the whole Bible. The whole thing – even the covers'. There was not necessarily the easy warmth here that you could find in other places, but we were about a mission.

At this time, we were reaching out to drug addicts and petty criminals. They would come to the home, and some we would be with as they came off the drugs, with all the withdrawal symptoms that entailed. So what I lived through at Ingleby Road was a full experience of discipleship. Len had a down-to-earth manner, and he was not into the theoretical but the application. We were ministering and serving together, but we were reflecting, arguing and learning as well.

There was an interesting demarcation of roles or, maybe it would be better to call it, a recognition of gifting. At this time, I was good at connecting people, so I would literally find people on the street and bring them into the home and sometimes the church meetings. But then Len would take over. He would teach, challenge, pray with them. He had such faith and saw amazing things. He was never fazed by anyone I brought in – which probably related to his earlier life as the local tough. We had different giftings and anointings and they complemented each other perfectly. This, then, was team: not sameness, but togetherness.

This is very close to the picture of discipleship that we see laid out in the Bible: apprenticeship; learning on the job; reflecting; being challenged; looking at your whole life (not just what you want to talk about). Proximity is key.

Our pastor at Bethel Church in Dagenham, Mr Webb, invited me to go with him on a week's evangelism crusade to another town. We went door to door, and ran open air meetings and an evening gospel meeting. Mr Webb would show me first and observe me as I took a turn, and then he took time to critique my approach and correct where I had gone astray. It was a very effective learning experience and a good example of apprenticeship/discipleship.

Another example of active apprenticing was with a national evangelist. He was a human dynamo – his work rate was tremendous, and he had such faith to see things happen, prayers answered, people healed. He took me with him on a crusade, and at the end of the first week he surprised me and, I suspect, the host church by announcing that I was to be leading all the meetings and events the next week, including a children's crusade and youth meetings. He would be leaving me to it as he went on to another location. Essentially I 'stood under his anointing'. He told me how to do it, prayed for me, I obeyed and things happened! Jesus had the same pattern with his disciples, they saw him in action then he sent them out to do the same with instructions about how they would go. The week with this evangelist left a deposit in me and I grew in faith and expectation.

You have to be near to people to see what they are really like. Often what is bandied around as discipleship is really accountability conversations — it's a confessional chat, and there is not much activity going on alongside those conversations. Of course, this is valid in itself. But with apprenticeship, when you hit your thumb with the hammer (i.e. when there is true pressure), what is in you will come out. There is no opportunity to rationalise your response before you feed back to your disciples — they are right there hearing your cry of pain and probably other things as well!

> *'When Jesus saw his ministry drawing huge crowds, he climbed a hillside. Those who were <u>apprenticed to him</u>, the committed, climbed with him. Arriving at a quiet place, he sat down and taught <u>his climbing companions</u>.'*
>
> — **Matt. 5:1–2, MSG** (emphasis added)

We see in the Message version that as Jesus sits down to teach on the Beatitudes in the Sermon on the Mount, 'disciples' is translated as 'apprentices' and then 'climbing companions'. That sense of journeying together, of learning from the teacher as we face different circumstances, is — I believe — a true picture of discipleship. Relationship at Len and Elsie's was developmental. Theirs was a place to grow.

So this is what I started to see church life could be: not just about meetings; relationship being at the core of life; a place of welcome and rest; a place to gather and a place to grow.

If we are set to advance and develop, we have to be ready to hear what God is saying to us individually and corporately. This means we need to be learning and reviewing at all times – in teaching it is called being a 'reflective practitioner'. That is how we need to be as a body and as followers of Christ.

We are not called to live according to either tradition or convention, but to die to self, learn from history and live by the revelation of God's word.

Eat the meat, spit out the bones

If we are intending to make a dent on the world, advance the Kingdom of God and be available to be avenues for God's blessing, we will have to stick our necks out. I think this is about our heart position and the resulting action – it's not just about getting the 'right word' from God, but doing something with it. It is not sufficient to know; we have to be committed to do. It seems obvious that if we sense that God is saying we need to go, we should go!

When we have a revelation, it should change the way we operate: we should not despise our former selves, but neither should we be stuck in tradition. We are on a journey, and we trust we are moving from 'glory to glory' (2 Cor. 3:18). If we stayed where we were, in the revelation of that time, we are not being true to what God is giving us – and yet we don't throw the baby out with the bathwater. The first love we have for Christ is something that is commented on in the Bible: we are told to return to our first love, not to despise it. As they grow up, teenagers have a tendency to make fun of the games and the toys that just a few years before they were enthralled with. There is no room for this in our walk with God: we must nurture our first love, but not stay in a childlike understanding.

> *When I was a child, I talked like a child, I thought like a child, I reasoned like a child. When I became a man, I put the ways of childhood behind me.*
>
> — 1 Cor. 13:11

It has often been the case that those we have shared with – often through our work overseas with LifeLine Network International[3], but also sometimes individuals and churches in the UK – have said, 'We love the teaching, the revelation you have. It has affected our way of seeing things… but we are not willing to put it into practice… just yet.' What a strange response! If the doctor tells us what to do to get better, we would want to take the medicine and move on – but so often people are not willing to do this. Of course, this is often because the medicine itself is not tasty; it is costly and uncomfortable, but it is what is needed for change and to move forward. Often, then, the churches and individuals who seem to have drawn much from us have been unwilling to pay the personal price. Funnily enough, I am not talking about a price in financial terms: in fact, at times people have been very keen to pay a financial fee – but not one that is likely to mean a change in their character. As a result of this simple, biblical message – which sometimes contradicts religious tradition and practice – we have been banned from relating to particular individuals, churches and countries.

A friend once said that what you suffer for, you become more passionate about. We have certainly suffered for the message of 'loving one another', and I am more passionate about this revelation of truth than I was 40 years ago. This is why the scripture 'Blessed are those … whose hearts are set on pilgrimage' is so important to us. We cannot stop here – we have a promise to fulfil. Why would we look at the Promised Land and then happily set up camp on the wrong side of the Jordan?

There was a young man who had been part of our youth work for many years, who decided to leave the church and go to another one down the road. There seemed to be no real negative reason for this, so Daniel met with him just to understand what was going on. He told Daniel how he appreciated what LifeLine did and how we had cared for and nurtured him, 'But I need to go somewhere where there are lower expectations of me.' What a sorry state of affairs – for that church to some extent, but more so for him, wanting a place of less challenge. We prayed him on his way and endeavoured to keep a door open. He went through a rocky period but is now connected with another church community.

---

3   See glossary for more information.

If we are set to advance and develop, we have to be ready to hear what God is saying to us individually and corporately. This means we need to be learning and reviewing at all times – in teaching it is called being a 'reflective practitioner'. That is how we need to be as a body and as followers of Christ.

We need to beware of fads and traditions, which look like shortcuts but really are long diversions from God's routes. In the excellent book *Love, Acceptance and Forgiveness*,[4] Jerry Cook speaks of the dual dangers of these. Fads are very hard to avoid – they could be called the fashions of the day, what is 'in', what is 'happening'. The problem is that following fads betrays the fact that you have no underlying philosophy or vision for the church. You are likely to pick up on the shiny new thing because that's what everyone else is doing.

One summer in the 1990s, at a gathering for young people, there was a sudden appearance of 'prayer sticks' in the hands of earnest youngsters. It's not quite clear where this phenomenon came from, but the result was a lot of thumping of the sticks on the ground while people were praying. No real harm there, but the especially earnest would swirl the sticks in the air, which caused a distraction for others when they were faced with real or perceived danger.

What is the danger of fads and traditions? Well, a fad becomes a distraction: it has no real purpose other than being fashionable, and as such we relate to it like a magpie attracted to something shiny rather than something useful. We can want shiny new things and miss out on God's purpose for us. A tradition, on the other hand, becomes a blockage in the mind, and can often be linked to legalism. It is something that has to be 'done right' or we will miss out. We have backslidden! Tradition and legalism say that the gospel of grace is not enough; to get salvation I need to do these additional things. Hence we are saying, 'Jesus, nice try! But you haven't done enough – I need to add some stuff. Your sacrifice and resurrection are not enough for salvation.' Falling into traditions means following practices that are born out of comfort and what has happened before, rather than that which God has for us now.

---

[4] Cook, J. with Baldwin, S. (1979). *Love, Acceptance and Forgiveness: Equipping the Church to be Truly Christian in a Non-Christian World.* Ventura, CA: Regal Books.

Daniel and the team at FaithAction[5] had another experience of 'fad-itis'. At a conference they had been asked to run a seminar stream on faith-based community action. At the end of their session, an elderly minster approached and said, 'Wonderful stuff this community service… but I'm afraid I've not got time for it – we've just started a food bank.' It was as if he had just taken a project off the shelf, without any true understanding of what that project was there for; he just wanted to do it because it was 'the thing to do'. So when he said that he did not have time for community social action, he missed the understanding that this was exactly what he was already doing.

This means our learning and reflection are very important. We have to 'chew on the meat and spit out the bones'. The examples that follow are stories from my formative years in the Pentecostal church.

Just turn on the tap

The scene was set for a dynamic night for me – and I was just trying to slip away! (It's funny how we sometimes get a bit nervous. Any way in which we can set people at ease is to be welcomed.) Pastor Webb, had got wind that although I had been around in the church for a while, I had not yet received the baptism of the Holy Spirit. I had planned to avoid him and slip off at the end of the meeting. However, he saw me at the start and invited me into his office before the meeting. Busted! God knew what he was doing. I had become averse to what I saw as the emotionalism in my parents' church, and so I had expected the pastor to use the meeting to 'soften me up', and make me more ready to respond. When he invited me into his office before the meeting, without any hype, I was disconcerted. I wasn't really prepared for an encounter with God – I had just taken the rush hour train from the City back to my parents' home in Hoddesdon, Hertfordshire, and then jumped in the car to drive to Dagenham for this meeting. I was not expecting much. There was no emotional build up.

I had met him many times before; in fact, as a young man I did not fully appreciate some of the ways in which he had welcomed me – these only occurred to me in later life. For instance, he invited me back there one night when he was about to have his tea. He asked me if I had

---

5 See glossary for more information.

eaten and, when I said I hadn't, suddenly there was half a meat pie in front of me. He had given me half of his dinner – and there was I, well fed and off home to mum who would always ensure there was food on the table – while he as widower had only this meagre meal, and now I was eating half of it.

Anyway, on this particular night there was nothing else on the table other than me! Or so I thought. Mr Webb went to the tap and turned it on. 'You see how easy it is,' he said, 'You just turn it on. That's how it is with the Holy Spirit – He comes and fills us as easy as turning on a tap.' There was no fanfare, no hype – much as I was expecting some; he just prayed for me and I was filled.

While I was at this church we had a visit from a team sent by David Wilkerson (author of *The Cross and the Switchblade*). I was to show them around, and they asked me to take them to the worst place in London. So off we went to Soho! What happened next surprised me. The method of street evangelism that I was used to was based on the idea of 'reaching' as many as possible. This was a kind of evangelical 'hit and run': tell the gospel message to as many as possible as quickly as possible – snatch people from hell, 'get 'em saved!' Our philosophy of church was as a holy ghetto, hanging on for Jesus to come quick before we succumb and backslide. So when this American team arrived in Soho, I was expecting noise and action as they tried to attract a crowd and get as many people to hear their message as possible. It wasn't to be that way. They started to wander around as if they were looking for someone specific. Eventually they approached one prostitute and spent time talking with her. They were being 'led by the Spirit'. There was no hype or human effort, or emotionalism – they were listening for God's direction. It was a powerful lesson for me about living in the power of the Holy Spirit.

I learned so much from that church and from Pastor Webb, but there were also things I learned not to do. The baptism of the Holy Spirit and the culture of sacrificial and generous giving was the meat; you will see later that there were also some 'bones' to be spat out.

I cut my teeth in Christian ministry in the 1960s, with the drug scene that was ruining the lives of many in our part of London. Then, as now, there were some pretty shady characters involved with the consumption and supply of heroin. A number of them came to faith, but they did not always express this in the way that people in the church expected. They did not wait for the Sunday evening gospel service, for one thing.

One lad, Norman, marched down to the front in the middle of the service, raised his hand high up in the air and lay down prostrate on the floor in front of everyone. The other addicts had said of Norman, 'Don't waste your time on him' – he was a prize fighter, and rough. But when he came to faith, he would often cry out 'Gawd bless Gawd!' He had experienced a total turnaround, and even learned to read supernaturally – he couldn't read and then suddenly he could! However, one of the best events for Norman was when he turned up to a meeting with a huge grin on his face. What was it? He had just come to the meeting on the bus, and for the first time he had paid his fare. It was one of the many transformations we saw.

Most of those who were responding were unkempt, looked not very well, and were not very clean. Our pastor had some little religious traits, and this meant he could sometimes be distracted by outward appearance, which then blunted his potential. For example, there was one of the dealers who wanted to visit. He was always very smartly dressed and 'together'. After he came in, my pastor drew me aside and said, "This is better, John – let's see if you can get more upstanding young men like him in." Of course, this chap was manipulative and exploitative, and the reason he was so well dressed was not because of honest toil. Many who came with me to church were small-time criminals, but this one was not so small-time: he had been involved with serious crime and had managed to get away with it.

On one occasion I had reached out to a homeless man and brought him to our church meeting. As the service came to an end I saw the limitations of what I had to give. All I could do was offer him a meeting, a religious service. And now here we were, about to tip him back on the street, leaving behind an empty building. It seemed that what I was peddling fell well short of God's heart. In the end I did the only thing I could think to do: I took him to the fish and chip shop, got him the largest portion of food that money could buy, and left him with that. He was happy enough – but was not Christian life about more than meetings?

It was about this time that I decided to buy an ice cream one Sunday. As I tucked in, the thought came to me: 'You've really lost it now – this is a clear sign that you are backsliding!' Yet I knew that my heart had never felt so close to God. I didn't feel that I was moving away from God, but towards him. What I was moving away from was the sort of legalism I had been part of since I was a child, which meant that it was 'sinful' to kick a football on a Sunday, to buy anything or to do anything that looked like work. For some reason, those who read the papers on a Monday were exempt, even though those papers were prepared on a Sunday. And of course the minister himself, who worked like a Trojan on a Sunday, was also excused!

At the same time, I started to go to some events run by anointed leaders of that time. At these events there was something different: I cannot really remember if there was anything about the format of the meetings themselves that was different, but there was a different result. I felt refreshed in my innermost being; my spirit was ministered to. This was not the emotionalism I had grown up in, nor was it the intellectual exercise I had come across in many traditional denominations; this was different. There was a wholeness and an expectation that the whole of us should be part of Christian life: not just the emotions or intellect, but the spirit as well.

A number of us were involved in putting together youth camps. Things went very well. Young people made commitments to Christ; there was healing and people were set free; and we also baptised in water. But on our return, the leader of the group got into a whole lot of trouble. Why? Well, this was not the way things were done! People got saved in the gospel service on a Sunday night, and they got baptised by the church leaders! There was a time and place for everything, and it certainly wasn't at a camp run by young adults.

The result was that I realised that church life was something beyond meetings and traditions. I was hungry for this, and I would take the good stuff from those who had nurtured me, but I would leave behind what was dross. My spirit could be ministered to, not just the emotions or the intellect. This was truly life changing.

What I learned from my early experiences is that people and their messages are a mixed bag. I am so grateful for those who invested in me when I was young. They had their understanding and tried to be true to that. You cannot live someone else's faith; you have to live what God has given you, with all sincerity.

By the way, beware of the flesh here, acting in accordance with 'my emotions' or 'my preferences'. I have often found that people hear what they want to hear – they hear selectively. If someone thinks that they are hearing from God that they should go in a certain direction, and that direction is characterised by death to self and preferring others, that seems to chime more with the word of God than the kind of direction that would not require this high calling of Christian life. Thus while I think that God's calling is the best for us, it seems to me that there is always a cost. If I persuade myself that what I want is what God is telling me to do, with no cost, change, preferring of others or carrying of my cross, have I just assumed that Christ is a spiritual waiter, and not Lord of all? Is that really God's will, or is it just me wrapping my desire up in fancy language so no one can counter it?

When Old Thompson prayed for China there was something different about it. The thing is, he didn't pray for China as we would describe it — he would say a few words of prayer, stammered out, and then he would weep for the nation, the people and the church. It was uncomfortable and awkward.

God uses those who are available and tuned in to Him, not those who feel they have it all together.

Old Thompson

At the Pentecostal church in Dagenham where I was first discipled, the missionary prayer meeting was the worst attended of all the meetings we had. In those days and in that congregation, we prided ourselves on meeting attendance, and would talk of 'supporting the meeting' – a strange concept, as surely the meeting, like any structure, is there to support the people and not the other way round. At that point we had a view of the 'architecture' of church that was more structural, organisational and hierarchical, and less about real relationship. We didn't see all of these things as being tools to strengthen the people in their true mission, which is to demonstrate to the world what God is like – to be a *witness*. However, it was in this rather odd meeting that a seed of revelation was planted in me.

As the few faithful gathered, people would pray for the world, and I mean that literally. They would start praying for Britain and work their way gradually around the globe, coming back to finish in the UK again, like a religious Phileas Fogg for what seemed like 80 days per prayer. Why was this? I suspect it was partly because of our limited understanding: something in us meant that we felt we ought to pray for those overseas, but we were not really clear why. So we covered everywhere, like a shopping list where you don't know if you need the things on the list but you think you had better buy them just in case.

I know of a missionary at this time, who recalls receiving packages from home containing all sorts of oddities, the meanest of which were second-hand, dried-out teabags. 'Treat 'em mean and keep 'em keen' seemed to be the unofficial policy of the church when it came to the remuneration and support of Christian workers. Missions were important, but we didn't really know why – we were not operating from a point of revelation-induced conviction or relational connection.

I think that something of the issue behind this attitude to the work of missionaries was linked to a partial understanding of our mission on earth. Our language led us to view 'the lost' as targets on an 'evangelism production board': we had not grasped the idea of 'Your kingdom come on earth'. Rather, we were focused on escaping earth for heaven, walking on streets of gold and knocking back cups flowing with milk and honey! I am not saying that everyone thought like this, but certainly I came to realise that this was underlying my thinking. Change was to come to me, but from a most unlikely direction.

'Old Thompson' attended the missionary prayer meeting without fail. This was the 1960s and Old Thompson was not what we would have called 'cool'. It was the era of the Beatles, the Rolling Stones, and so on: we knew about cool. Although – let's face it – we were Pentecostals in Dagenham: we weren't exactly cool either, but all the same, he took lack of cool to new depths. He had a speech impediment but, even without this limitation, he was not an articulate or intellectual man. However, when Old Thompson prayed for China there was something different about it. The thing is, he didn't pray for China as we would describe it – he would stammer out a few words of prayer, and then he would weep for the nation, the people and the church. It was uncomfortable and awkward. There was so much we didn't know about China at that time: the Communist Revolution had taken place in the late 1940s and westerners and missionaries had all been thrown out of the country. Christianity was oppressed and we didn't know if there were any Christians left. What's more, the Cultural Revolution had started and with all the devastation and purges that were part of that, news was even more difficult to get hold of. But here was Old Thompson weeping for China.

What we were to discover years later was that there was a great revival happening in China, with many turning to Jesus. The church had been growing even as it was severely oppressed, and thus Old Thompson had been on the frontline – a prayer warrior, immersed in the heart of God for those people, tuned into God's frequency; not articulate, not cool, and hardly able to get a word out, but having a heart bursting for God's will on earth.

What I started to learn was that godly compassion does not necessarily come from what we see with human eyes, but is more about being in tune with the Father – tuned in with spiritual ears. In that sense it is more about the 'heart position' than the insight, knowledge or abilities of the hearer. Over the years I have seen and sometimes been part of any number of clever ideas and schemes – group structures, evangelism methods, worship approaches. But what we have learned by the grace of God is that a heart turned to His – an internal throbbing for Him – is the best way to receive direction and guidance and His voice is the best guide. This is what Old Thompson had.

The greatest example we have of being led by Godly compassion is Jesus. We know He did only what He saw the Father do (John 4:19, 12:49). In John chapter 5 we have a most intriguing account of Jesus's ministry. He is in Jerusalem and comes upon the pool at Bethesda. A great many disabled people are gathered there, as when the waters are stirred the first one into the pool gets healed. There is one man who has been waiting for 38 years, but he does not have anyone to help him into the pool, and so he has not been healed. Jesus heals him. (The religious folk get distracted by the fact that this activity is taking place on the Sabbath – oh Lord, save us from the distraction of form and rules rather than celebrating your divine power!) What sticks out to me in this story is what didn't happen; all those who were in need but weren't healed. Jesus, doing only what the Father gave Him to do, must have more or less stepped over other people in great need. He was not distracted by what he could see, but instead was guided by the heart that God had set in Him.

With the various fundraising campaigns we see on posters and TV, the phenomenon of 'compassion fatigue' has arisen. We see images of neglected children, sad-looking animals, appealing and weeping celebrities, asking for just a bit of our attention and an offer of 'just so many pounds a month', as if our compassion could be provoked and then gently assuaged and packed away with a quick exchange of money. I am not against charity and these appeals, but I am against the idea that our humanity can be so compartmentalised. This is because our minds cannot sift through all the images and respond to them all. Surely if you or I had been at the pool of Bethesda we would not have been able to pick out that one man, as Jesus did: we would have been overwhelmed and probably no use to anyone in the task before us. I want to have my ears tuned to God's voice, His nudges. Having a heart that hears is a good way of ensuring that the resources He has given us can grow and that we avoid responding only out of human compassion. Otherwise we can be like the third servant in the parable of the talents (Matt. 25:14), who cannot see what to do and so does nothing.

It would be wrong to think that we should be cut off from the world around us, not troubled by the state of other people's lives. In fact, I think we should be 'hyper-sighted', rather than just seeing with our human eyes, often led by the fads and interests of TV news directors or the editors and owners of newspapers and news websites. No – we should see things in a prophetic way (that is how God sees things, with eternal perspective and wisdom), in a godly-compassionate way. That is one of the reasons we were able to join with the late Richard Cole in his work in Sierra Leone[6]. Initially this was a little heard-of conflict, its atrocities only briefly touching our news stands, as the focus in the UK at the time was on the various political intrigues of early 1990s politics, the exchange rate mechanism, the Euro and other 'first world problems'. We were brought to the work in Sierra Leone not because of a need, but because of a God-initiated relationship. We did not see with our eyes, but felt the call of God with our hearts. Why else would our seemingly insignificant group in east London join in on the mission of helping to rebuild a nation?

Seeing things the way God sees them had a particular touchdown in my life when I was still working in the City. I prayed what could be considered a foolish prayer. I prayed that God would enable me for a moment to see people as he saw them. I warn you now, don't ask this unless you are ready for a painful and life-changing experience. There I was, walking along a street in the City of London, busy with other workers hurrying about their working day, when suddenly what I saw changed. No longer the neutral faces of fellow commuters, but the expressions of pain and anguish of a people lost and separated from their Father in heaven, lives broken and laid bare. A moment beforehand I had seen the outside, the presented image of a City worker, and the next moment I saw them with spiritual x-ray vision. Their lostness made my heart cry out and I could hardly continue my journey. It was such a vivid experience that even now, over 40 years later, I cannot

---

6   See the chapter 'Kingdom without Borders' for more of the Sierra Leone story.

recount this experience without reliving the wealth of emotion and yes, compassion, that God has for His world – a godly compassion that does not fatigue.

You see, what I learned from Old Thompson was availability: it is not those who feel they have it 'all together', but those who are available – and thus tuning into God – whom He will use. Isaiah 6 describes the journey so well: we are not worthy, and not even our lips could speak for God, yet He has purified us so that in the end we can say 'Here am I – send me!' (Isa. 6:8). That attitude and position has sent us to many places and arenas where what we have been able to bring has been ground-breaking – whether by the potency of our fellowship and relationship with each other, or influencing policy and seeking to change nations for good. This is not because we are especially spiritual: we are certainly not more gifted or richer than most. But we have made ourselves available, and we have a high expectation that this could lead us anywhere God would have us go.

Old Thompson was not the coolest, but God used him to be a part of what He was doing on the earth. What an accolade – to be a co-worker with Christ, not 'cool', but chosen.

Here I was, looking at the terrible result of a 7.2 magnitude quake, among the brothers and sisters we were joined with. Everywhere we went there were piles of clothing lying heaped in the rain and mud. However, no one was poorly dressed; that was not the need.

Relationship cannot happen without a proximity of heart, or a face-to-face proximity – not just by Skype or FaceTime. Caring goes way beyond what you can see on the surface, or even what is presented. You have to be close enough to see, observe, question, love and serve appropriately.

As I stood with piles of clothes at my feet...

Everything fell into sharp relief as I stood with piles of clothes at my feet. I was in a village near Naples in Italy, at the request of Giovanni, a local pastor we had known for some time. Italy had been struck by a series of earthquakes, and there was much devastation. Our hearts went out to the people there and as a church we wanted to respond to the needs of our family in Christ.

We made contact: 'What can we do?' In the midst of their desperation a call came through that would change how we would build church. 'Just come and see!' was the answer. So here I was, looking at the terrible result of a 7.2 magnitude quake, among the brothers and sisters we were joined with. Everywhere we went there were piles of clothing lying heaped in the rain and mud. However, no one was poorly dressed; that was not the need. It was housing that was the problem, not clothing. So I asked – why all these clothes? Giovanni answered that they had been donated by churches and charities across Europe. People had seen the news and devastation on TV and sent clothes. It was an impulsive response: at best ignorant, at worst more about cathartic release, focused more on the donor than the needs of the recipient. They collected second-hand surplus and here it was, piles of clothing, while what the people needed was building materials to rebuild their homes and their lives.

No one had asked what was really needed. It was a mindset whereby people in a far-removed state could decide what was to happen on the ground and dispatch it in a single deed of social action – job done, conscience assuaged. This was aid without cost. I don't mean financial cost, although that was probably minimal; this was a donation that was uninvolved, disconnected, self-serving and soulish.

This experience highlighted to me things that we had walked through in the first years of church life (by this time, we had left the Pentecostal church and were part of a new house church, which was to become LifeLine Church[7]): real relationship, expressed through shared life and serving – not as a means to an end, but a state of being. And this kind of serving was an expression of love, rather than just to get a job done.

I did not realise it at the time, but this visit to Giovanni became a pattern for how we would work overseas. In many ways it was not to be very different from how we would operate at home. LifeLine Network International should never be made up of those who are the 'done to' on the one hand, and the 'doers' on the other. We are brothers and sisters together; together 'we have the mind of Christ' (1 Cor. 2:16). 'There is neither Jew nor Gentile, neither slave nor free, nor is there male and female, for <u>you are all one</u> in Christ Jesus' (Gal. 3:28; emphasis added). You see the Bible, in ancient times, had a picture of equality before it was in vogue in our modern times. When we went to Italy, we went to visit our brethren; we didn't go to dispense our ministry upon the 'poor wretches' – we were visiting family! Once we were there, we decided together how we would respond to the situation. You could call it intelligence gathering, but I think that has the wrong tone. Their heart's desire was to be joined with others; ours was to be with our brothers and sisters in their time of need, to cry with those who cry (Rom. 12:15). And praise God! We also get to rejoice with those who rejoice.

This is all about proximity. Relationship cannot happen without a proximity of heart, and I would say there needs to be a face-to-face proximity as well. When you are on the phone to someone or using Skype or FaceTime, it is harder to 'notice' things. What is going on behind what is being presented? I remember visiting one family in the church. All seemed okay as far as what was being said, but when I asked the husband about the wellbeing of the wife, it opened up a route into what was really amiss. Let's not beat around the bush here: I did not ask an airy question about 'wellbeing'. I asked, in a caring way, 'Why does your wife appear careworn, bedraggled and untidy?' What a cheek! How rude to say this! Yes, you could view it that way – forc-

---

7 See glossary for more information.

ing my standards onto another. Or you could say that it was a way of caring that went beyond the surface, beyond what was presented, in a desire to see a dear couple become all that God intended.

You can't really see, smell and feel what is going on from a distance. You have to be close enough that you will notice something. I have often gone to visit people overseas not to minister, but just to see them and to be with them in times of difficulty. The church in the UK has made this possible by releasing me to go, and my family has had to bear the brunt of this. There have been countless holidays interrupted so that I could be with people – a Florida holiday interrupted so I could attend a funeral, and a trip to Disney cancelled so that our family could be with a family with a dying child. But you know what? We have never regretted giving ourselves in this way.

Love is primarily demonstrated through practical acts of service. And if there was any doubt of the need for proximity in relationships, there is no doubt when it comes to serving. You have to be close to serve, or you are in danger of being like that distant aunt who diligently sends through scented handkerchiefs each Christmas, or like churches who send clothes when what is needed are bricks and builders.

Serving has become our default response. I am speaking of LifeLine Church here: we have a fantastic group of people ready and raring to give and serve. One of my jobs as a church leader is to protect the people from being taken advantage of, so ready are they to give of themselves. As a leadership we endeavour to give guidance on serving, and we continue to teach on the subject – not because it is a weakness among us, but because it is a strength. 'When it's raining, pray for rain'[8] is something we often say: we want to celebrate and expand the good things that God is doing with us. What is sometimes more of a challenge is to discern between different types of possible response, so that we are serving not just physical needs, but emotional and spiritual needs as well.

---

[8] Jesus says He only does what He sees the Father doing (John 5:19); Zech. 10 speaks of the seasons that God operates in and determines.

More and more I see serving as the glue of relationship, but that glue is more than a translucent substance that sticks things together. Serving is more a luminous, fluorescent and glowing glue, which shows the potency of our community relationships. Without serving, relationship has a somewhat hollow ring.

> *'In the same way, let your good deeds shine out for all to see, so that everyone will praise your heavenly Father.'*
> — Matt. 5:16, NLT

Serving is the lifeblood of a relational community. It puts the 'shared' into 'shared life'. This was demonstrated again and again by Jesus, who first had disciples that they might be with him (Mark 3:14), but left us with poignant examples of serving.

We have many great stories of serving and sacrificial giving. God has blessed us with a community of people who are so keen and prompt to act that there does not need to be a nagging or cajoling – it just happens. My daughter-in-law had suffered with a pregnancy-related condition, so for a series of months she was unable to walk properly, and with two small children and a new-born baby this was very difficult. To supplement what her husband could do, there was always someone from the church on hand to help with childcare during the day, and meals were provided for an extended period – but to top it off she noticed that her hanging basket had been replenished with flowers. That 'going beyond the need' to bless those we serve is typical of the heart of the people I serve. To this day we don't know who did this, but we know it was done in the name of Jesus.

After my fall, a retired senior hospital consultant in the church came every day to administer the injections I needed. That makes sense, doesn't it – he was using his medical background to serve. But it doesn't explain why he taxied me to all my physio appointments. It certainly doesn't explain why he then cut the lawn for me. He fed it and took on any number of garden tasks. Never before (or since) has that garden been so well cared for – and nor have I, for that matter!

One of the best pictures of serving and commitment was displayed by a brother who was to be teaching our Doulos[9] course on one island in the Caribbean. He skilfully arranged his teaching around his dialysis appointment on another island. He arrived more or less fresh from the hospital, but his action spoke louder than words. Why? His topic that day was 'Commitment'. Another brother delayed his hip replacement so that he would be free to serve with the children's work. We like to put our beliefs into action. A number of years ago there was a bout of illness in our house and Dawn had been quite ill. There was a knock at the door, and in walked a sister from church with a saucepan of peeled potatoes rather than a bunch of flowers. She had seen the need and fulfilled it.

Availability is important in serving. One of the families in the church contacted me, distraught: their autistic son had broken away from the family as they were getting into the car and had run off into the local park. They couldn't catch him and they couldn't leave their other children. I placed a couple of calls and within minutes every entrance of the park was covered and parties of brothers and sisters were fanning out across the park to retrieve this lad.

For a number of years, the whole church would troop off in May to a campsite near Weymouth for a church holiday. No meetings – just a chance to be away together. We had great weather, once or twice! Once there was a sudden storm in the middle of the day, while many people were out on various excursions. The wind whipped up and tents started to rip up and blow away. A call went out, and it was quite something to see the people who were still on site streaming from all directions to a central point to rescue those tents. It was quite amusing to see people arrive back with anxious faces later that day, to discover all their belongings packed into cars, when they had expected them to have blown away.

Relationship and serving are of course part of laying down our lives for one another. We had a particular demonstration of this one summer when we were running a kids' and youth programme in a local park. During the early evening, a group of teenagers armed with screwdrivers started to threaten those who had gathered to watch the bands that were playing. There was a scuffle as a number of our church members

---

9   See glossary for more information.

dived into harm's way to subdue the youths and disarm them. It seems amusing now thinking about a squirming young man who was being sat upon by one of our burlier members, but it had all been quite dangerous — yet there was no hesitation when it came to risking life and limb.

Leadership must be viewed through the prism of serving. If we are to be leaders as Jesus is a leader, there is no place for being separated from the people by location or title. When visiting a community overseas for the first time, I am often asked what I should be called — Bishop, Apostle, Reverend, Pastor? I reply 'John', and this seems to create some disappointment at first, but we get over that.

This attitude of leaders as servants should not lead to disrespect, because the Bible says,

> *'Obey your leaders and follow their orders. They watch over your souls without resting, since they must give to God an account of <u>their service</u>. If you obey them, they will do their work gladly; if not, they will do it with sadness, and that would be of no help to you.'*
> — **Heb. 13:17, GNT** (emphasis added)

However, it does fly in the face of the worldly approach of puffing a person up and not recognising that we follow a 'Servant King'.

Relationship, serving and proximity really come into play when you open your home up to have someone live with you. This is something many of us have done: not taking on a lodger, but adding someone to the family. This means that when they move out, they don't leave the family — they are still connected, just like natural kids. We have had many live with us over the years but one story comes to mind.

We had one young woman come to stay who had what I think we could safely describe as 'alternative' attitudes, compared with us. She was feminist, very left wing, dungaree wearing and opinion spouting. She was a hoot! She came to stay for a month and ended up being with us for ten years.

We have never been all that focused on fashion, but her dress code said something about her. It wasn't particularly showy or radical — in fact, when we had a break-in, she was somewhat offended to discover that the burglar had not found anything in her room to steal.

After a while our proximity started do some work in her. Dawn and I were on the stairs one day heading up to bed when the young woman asked, 'Is there a problem with what I wear?' She tells us now that her heart sank with what happened next. We sat down on the stairs. Her passing question was going to get a full response. We talked for a while about different things – attitudes, reactions – and she started to change: it wasn't all about her wardrobe, but the attitudes behind that wardrobe. Our focus was on what was going on inside of her, not on what she was wearing. But we had to be close enough to sit on the stairs. It was the relationship proximity which allowed us to serve her with some truth that she would not have heard otherwise.

Of course, relationship and serving are the bits we can do, empowered by the Spirit living in us. They are a kind of 'life-song', but there are times that God just gets involved obviously and directly, adding a very special harmony.

Mark McGrath was visiting us from New Jersey and speaking at our Sunday gathering in a local secondary school hall. We have known Mark for over 30 years and he has been ministering in the UK for even longer, particularly in the south-west. Now each Sunday, a team of people start setting up the hall a number of hours before the rest of us arrive. One of the team this week was not well but, having given his apologies, he realised that he had our church banner which goes on the outside of the school to show passers-by that we are there. The banner was a bit of a joke among the team, as it seemed superfluous to setting up the meeting given that we just didn't get 'walk-ins'. However, this young man dragged himself from his sickbed, drove to the school, attached the banner and returned home to bed.

The meeting started and when Mark came to speak he told a remarkable story. A missionary who had returned to our local area for respite was in the congregation that day. His wife was pregnant and, having not slept well the night before, was resting at home with their young daughter. He was discouraged and low and decided to drive around that Sunday morning to see if he could spot a church to visit, for encouragement. He spotted the banner and came into the meeting. He had grown up in the church that his father pastored in the south-west, so imagine his surprise when he saw who was to speak that day: Mark McGrath, the American pastor who had ministered to his father's church for much of his childhood, and whom he hadn't seen for a number of years. He was recognising God's hand in guiding him to our community and connecting him again to a brother from thousands of miles away. However, it was Mark who spotted the factors at work here. He thanked the set-up team for their faithful service and making sure that the banner was up: it led his friend in, for there was no way he would have come into the building and received the blessing of seeing Mark if there had been no banner. The relationship and commitment that we shared was the foundation God used to bless a couple tired by their service. He provided Mark to be there at that very time, to show His sovereign acting and His desire to put the cherry on top! The main star of the story was asleep in bed, but we told him of his part when he recovered.

II
Discovering on the Job

When it comes to difficult issues around giving, tithes and offerings, it is often problems around trust and authority that lie at the root… people often have personal objections which show something about what is going on inside them.

Responsibility, authority and accountability have to sit together. Excellence is not to do with how much you have to spend or give, but the quality of the heart in the giving.

God wears out carpets

Time and time again we have learned the truth of the phrase 'Money is the great thermometer – it shows on the outside what is going on inside.' Jesus was not shy about speaking about money; in fact, he talked of nothing more often other than the Kingdom of God. So let us not be side-tracked into thinking that when we are looking at money, all we are really talking about are issues of tithing, offerings or greed.

Our attitude to money shows so much more about our attitudes to other things; really it has to do with our worldview. It reveals where our security lies, how we view God and how we view authority. It even shows how we think organisations should work, and how the operation of those organisations should relate to us as individuals, as well as to what degree we are willing to be open to others and their input and guidance. Are we really happy to engage with the fellowship of believers and 'shared life'?

So how we handle money – how we think of it and plan for it – gives a great insight into us. That has to be why it is a taboo subject around the dinner party table!

Daniel was based at a church in America for six months as part of his year out before university. Other than a brush with the Anglican high church in the UK while at school, as an 18-year-old this was the first time that he had seen the inner workings of any church other than LifeLine. The pastor was a long-term friend and invested in Daniel in the most generous way, giving him an opportunity – as a relative outsider – to come into the 'guts' of a large church and see what really went on. He made time every week to challenge Daniel on his doctrinal assumptions, and to study with him. Of course this led to a dual learning experience for Daniel, in terms of what he heard and of what he saw.

This church was led by a team of elders, the ministry team. There was also another group which gave input to the pastor and was drawn from the business community. This finance committee contained some of the most successful business people in the church – and thus some of the biggest givers. In fact, one of the members of the finance committee had been a pastor in another town and had initially been part of the ministry team; he had left that group but remained on the finance committee. He now ran a very successful business and was very generous to those in need in the church. However, there were some tensions within this set-up. It was good to benefit from some expertise in finance as an input to the direction of the church finances, but this situation had moved too far, such that it really was a case of 'he who holds the purse strings calls the shots'. The spiritual leadership was stunted by the checks and balances of the finance committee, and it appeared that a former elder was commanding influence through these mechanisms without adequate accountability.

This desire to balance authority and resource is more akin to the operation of secular powers than the principle laid out in Acts:

> *For there was not a needy person among them, for all who were owners of land or houses would sell them and bring the proceeds of the sales, and <u>lay them at the apostles' feet</u>, and they would be distributed to each as any had need.*
>
> — ACTS 4:34–35, **NASB** (emphasis added)

Responsibility, authority and accountability have to sit together. Far too often churches have engineered a situation in which the leaders have responsibility, but not the financial authority to enact that responsibility. At the heart of this is trust. We have to trust our leaders, recognising that they don't always get it right. No system or bureaucracy can ever replace trust and integrity.

The situation that Daniel came across in this church in the USA was very similar to what I had seen in my younger years in the life of the churches I was part of. These situations were not always focused on finances – but they often were. The selection and election of elders, the constitution and members' meetings seemed to create the backdrop of a frugal and 'tight' attitude towards church workers. And if we were going to be thrifty in our attitude towards Christian workers, we would certainly have a thrifty attitude to the rest of what we did as the church. Could we do it on the cheap? Was it a knock-off or below standard? Well, that's alright – it's only for the church, after all.

This lack of generosity – this miserly approach – is not becoming of the Kingdom of God or of followers of Jesus. I don't want waste, by any means, but I do want excellence. That's why an 'it'll do' attitude is not right. We pursue excellence: that is, doing the best with that which we have in our hands; we want to give generously, create top-quality events, give of ourselves with excellent hearts. You see, the end product is important, but our way of travelling is of greater importance. The disciples may well have quibbled about the woman who poured perfume on Jesus' feet (Mark 14), but no one was denying the quality of her heart.

One of the brothers whom we met early on in the house church movement demonstrated to me what it was like to be a channel for God's blessing, purpose and finance. We were visiting his home, where there was no washing machine, the carpets had seen better days, and there was obvious need. Yet he was buzzing about an offering he had just received when he was speaking at another church. He said to me that it was so good to get that offering at that time, as the next day a missionary passed through with a need and he was able to pass on the gift that had been given to him. The whole idea of not giving in order to get, but receiving in order to give, had a great impact on me.

The home has always been the primary place of our church life. Open homes are vital to 'living out' church, as was demonstrated by the early church. It is one of the features of the church that is perhaps most at risk: we like sacred space, not for altars and spiritual activity, but as a preserve of the idolatry of 'me'. The picture of Christ on the cross is a powerful image of vulnerable openness. It was with His arms wide open that He was to declare 'It is finished!' (John 19:30).

In the early days of our church some of us had homes, some had cars – we used what we had to serve 'the body'. For one of our gatherings in the home of one of the leaders, we had invited a visiting speaker, someone we respected and were seeking to learn from. After the meeting he drew us aside and said "God wears out carpets!" Well, the carpets in that home were indeed worn, but what did he mean? His point was – why did we not use the money we had in the church to bless this family and the group who met in their house with a new carpet? It was a revolutionary idea to use the money in the church to help someone in this way. It was a key part of our journey to have a radical approach to finance.

When my boys were very young, there came a time as they moved out of their cots when we needed to get new beds. Dawn had her heart set on a set of pine bunk-beds. Being the more cautious of us both, she pushed this desire out of her mind and started to look around for cheaper alternatives. After all, God said he would supply all our *needs*, not all our desires! But there came a change in our understanding. God is not a miser, and we received a gift and a clear prompt to get those beds. What this taught her was that God didn't want us to 'make do' – he is a generous God who wants the best for us, even stretching to the extravagance of pine bunk-beds!

Excellence is not to do with how much you have to spend or give, but the quality of the heart in the giving. When one young woman felt called to serve me, we didn't have a church office. We agreed she should do a typing course, and we got a typewriter, but there was no desk to type at. So she would type on her bed while kneeling on the floor. She also reduced her working hours to be available to serve me. This was a different form of excellence: she was available to serve with the tools we had at the time, and the thing that her 'hand found to do' (Eccles. 9:10). This is reflective of the 'widow's mite' (Luke 21:1–4): she was not able to give anything large and expensive but what she gave, she gave with excellence. The bunks came from a godly prompting, and this woman's heart of being available to serve was also a response to a prompting.

When it comes to difficult issues of giving, tithes and offerings, it is often problems around trust and authority that lie at the root (I am not going to explore the principles of tithes and offerings here, but needless to say I believe in both of them). What is noteworthy is not someone's doctrine on the issue, but the fact that people often have personal objections which show something about what is going on inside them, aside from any 'cloaking' doctrinal discussion. This is what we mean when we say that money is like a barometer, that it shows on the outside what is going on inside.

As with so many things, our starting point is so different from that of the western world we live in. The world says, 'This is my life – I need to protect it and stop outsiders from interfering. I have to protect myself, I have to work for my own security, I need insurance – a bargaining position – a nest-egg to protect me.' Essentially this is the position of an orphan: with no father or family to protect and nurture them, they are left to fend for themselves. This is not how we are called to live as children of a heavenly Father.

Instead our position is that we are involved in each other's lives – yes, open and vulnerable, not protected and isolated. We are involved in each other's decisions and choices, not because we are dictating from afar, but because we are close, we are committed, we have 'skin in the game', and as a community – a family – we will bear together the consequences of your life choices.

It is interesting that although the father in the story of the prodigal son (Luke 15) gave away half of what he had, by the time the younger son returned, he seemed no less wealthy than at the start. His openness did not put him into poverty. We have found that we have been richer for investing into each other. We may not always have felt flush with cash, but our open hand has been more profitable than a grasping one.

So are we without any checks and restrictions? By no means. I have always been very clear that I will not be involved in the pay review for my own support; there is a separate grouping that deals with my benefits. On the other hand, we take seriously our teaching on money, and we are careful not to fall into following 'fad' teachings just because something works for others. We strongly confront the 'prosperity doctrine'[10], which at its core has a wrong view of the gracious nature of God and continues to do such damage to Christians and the reputation of the church.

---

10 This is the erroneous doctrine that we should give in order to get.

Often some of the most dynamic stories of finance and provision happen in small settings within groups, or even anonymously. Our finance department gets continually blessed as they see how the church members give to one another anonymously, using the office as the conduit to convey money.

One such story happened within a small group in the early 1990s, a hard time financially in the UK. One couple with a young family had been suffering with poor rental accommodation. Their group had been praying about this for some time, when the leader decided to challenge them to back their prayers with action. If they were agreed that this situation was not right, and the mortgage offer this couple could muster fell well short of house prices, what should the group do? You see, we can easily get into praying about a problem, but leaving it on the plate of others. Prayer and action are powerful when they come together, when we recognise ourselves as God's tools and ministers on earth.

The group decided to engage practically with the issue, and they started to give sacrificially to make up the necessary deposit for the house. Savings were contributed; a new car was not bought; decorating was held off; the solicitor wanted to get in on the act and waived his fees – and, of course, relationships went to another level. £10,000 was needed, a huge sum at the time, and the group came up with £10,000 (making £12,000 with the solicitor's fees). One of the fathers of the couple, not in the church, worried throughout how they would pay everyone back (he couldn't understand it was simply a gift), so I suppose that was a witness as well. And remember, this was not a general church activity; this was one small group who were committed to one another, and it didn't stop there. They were involved again in the decorating when the keys were handed over, ripping up floors, merrily Artex-ing ceilings, painting, stripping paper, assembling furniture and so on. This was an investing of relationship, not 'fire and forget' donations.

Like much else in this book, stories of finance also become stories of relationship and commitment. As I have often said, when I give an offering to God, I am giving a piece of me in foldable form. In fact, this works with all giving, doesn't it? Unless we are very rich, when we give money we are giving of ourselves – there is often sacrifice involved. At various times we have made decisions as leaders that might not have seemed the most logical from a financial point of view, but were where we felt God was leading us. Before I was in full-time ministry and the church was on a precarious footing, one of our founding members and I took it in turn to pay the bills: one month he would do it and then next month I would. On another occasion, when I was full-time, the financial situation looked bleak again. One of the other leaders, who was not in full-time ministry, said, 'We as leaders chose this path together – it is not right for you to carry all the risk. For as long as you need it, half my salary is yours.' More than the financial reality, it felt good to know that we were committed to each other and the vision together – that someone had my back. This is far away from the mean mentality I saw in my youth.

When we look back now on some of the things we did 40 years ago — or to be honest just five years ago — we often remark that we were a bit crazy… It's easy to live in the good of it now, without remembering that these values and revelations were hard fought, sometimes against the established church denominations at the time, but more often against the selfish desires and behaviours and preferences of us as human beings.

By actively seeking to take on projects to serve one another, being in and out of each other's houses, you can 'share life'. By doing this you can start to rediscover what it means to be followers of Jesus like those in the early church.

So we buried the car

When we look back now on some of the things we did 40 years ago – or to be honest just five years ago – we often remark that we were a bit crazy. Why on earth did we go about things that way? In the re-telling of stories it's often hard to remember why we did things. It's more amusing to share what we did without explanation, but actually we did crazy things because we were deadly serious about the new understanding or revelation we had received. It was and is a precious thing – in fact sometimes I feel we are in danger of not cherishing what God has revealed to us. It's easy to live in the good of it now, without remembering that these values and revelations were hard fought, sometimes against the established church denominations at the time, but more often against the selfish desires and behaviours and preferences of us as human beings.

I have always been a firm believer in the spirit of Phil. 2:12: 'continue to work out your own salvation with fear and trembling' (ESV). This is one of those reinforcing verses about the nature of the priesthood of all believers: no one can do it for us – we need to work out our salvation, or 'Christ-life'. But the Bible brings truth to us in balance; as though no one sentence can ever sum up God's wisdom. Two ideas have to be held in happy tension. So although there is an emphasis on the individual, there is also much focus on the corporate, and more on relationship with God and with each other.

I've never liked the beach: sand, salt, sunburn – and in the UK, the inevitable downpour – don't appeal to me. This dislike I share with Daniel, but you cannot always have what you want. In the spirit of being together, we booked a number of trips as a church. Coaches picked people up from various locations around north-east London, and out we headed. On one occasion it was the beach at Walton, and it was a Saturday in the summer – what could go wrong? I can't remember if this was the trip when there was travel sickness on the coach and the coach driver had nothing to aid the clear-up and was generally unhelpful. Anyway, we arrived at the east coast, more or less in one piece. The coaches disgorged their contents of urban saints, and on to the beach we went, with very white legs in questionable shorts. Before defences could be erected the first drops of rain started. The cry went up, 'It's just a passing shower!' Surely this was tempting fate, as this was not a passing shower – this was a staying deluge. We were wet, and pretty miserable, but we were together and that was the point of the whole exercise.

The 1970s were an interesting time. Recycling had not become as sophisticated as it is today, and for a time it was costly to scrap an old car. One of our group had a car that was no good, but we did not want to shell out the money to scrap it. So one bright spark had an idea: 'I've got a big back garden – let's bury it there.' So there we all were, digging by hand a very big hole. It seemed a great solution at the time, but we really hadn't calculated how much earth we would have to move. However, once you start a task like this, you are committed and there is no going back, so on we pushed. As far as we know, to this day the car remains buried in a back garden in east London. What a surprise there will be for someone in years to come!

You can see the practical and economic reasons why we buried the car, but there was much more to it. We were in it together, we actively sought to take on projects to serve one another, we were in and out of each other's houses, we were seeking to 'share life'. We were focused on rediscovering what it meant to be followers of Jesus like those in the early church. We tuned in to the description of church in Acts 2:

> *They devoted themselves to the apostles' teaching and to fellowship, to the breaking of bread and to prayer. Everyone was filled with awe at the many wonders and signs performed by the apostles. All the believers were together and had everything in common. They sold property and possessions to give to anyone who had need. Every day they continued to meet together in the temple courts. They broke bread in their homes and ate together with glad and sincere hearts, praising God and enjoying the favour of all the people. And the Lord added to their number daily those who were being saved.*
>
> — Acts 2:42–47

This meant we buried a car and bought a giant vat of strawberry jam to share (which it turned out nobody liked). The idea was to save money, pool our resources, live in unity and have everything in common. We were intentional about living as they did in Acts. We continued to meet in homes even when we had access to bigger buildings, and for a time many of us had 'any driver' insurance so that we could make our cars available to each other.

I remember another time when our commitment to one another received a particular testing. I had left my career in the stock market to work full-time for the church. At this time, the church's financial outlook was not good. Among the elders, some were supported by the church and some were in full-time employment. Those of us who were supported proposed that we take a 10% cut. At this point one leader who was in employment said that if this was to be the case, then he would also take a 10% cut and offer that to the church for our support. All the others agreed. What a difference that made to all of us: it was commitment and relationship with bite. It was not theoretical – it was gritty, practical, and costly. And you know what? Things changed very quickly. We didn't have to take up the offer and none of us had to take a pay cut, but I know it was a commitment, a covenant between us which made a difference – and God honoured it. And it is a foundation stone for us, planted there in our early years… deeper than that car.

> *How good and pleasant it is*
>   *when God's people live together in unity!*
> *It is like precious oil poured on the head,*
>   *running down on the beard,*
> *running down on Aaron's beard,*
>   *down on the collar of his robe.*
> *It is as if the dew of Hermon*
>   *were falling on Mount Zion.*
> *For there the* LORD *bestows his blessing,*
>   *even life for evermore.*
>
> — Ps. 133:1–3

The place of the family home was to be an important basis for the direction and flavour of the church...This, coupled with the house church emphasis on relationship and home-focused activity, meant that the family home was always to be important.

Hospitality is hard to describe: more apparent in the results, the feeling that the recipient is left with. When people come into our sphere, cross the threshold of our lives, do they feel attended to? Do they feel part – or segregated? Is there generosity of resources and time?

Meals and Mars Bars

In the first few years of LifeLine Church, or North London Community Church as it was known then, I was praying and felt that God asked me a distinct question. Did I want to have a highly successful ministry, if it meant that my children would not be followers of Jesus? Or was I prepared for a less successful ministry, but one where I would see my three sons walk with God? I decided that what I wanted most was to have my boys walk with God, and this they are doing – with the added bonus that they are all involved alongside me in serving in LifeLine.

The place of the family home was to be an important basis for the direction and flavour of the church. You will recall how it was the three homes in my old church that made such an impression on me. This, coupled with the house church[11] emphasis on relationship and home-focused activity, meant that the family home was always to be important. It also means that the 'inner sanctum', that place of retreat from 'outside' work, be that secular or church-related, is vulnerable and open to abuse. But then again it also means it is open to blessing.

There were a number of things that we decided to institute to make the home an active part of all that we did and who we are. The boys were always able to come to us and speak to us, and they would come into meetings and see us. They learned as they grew that there were times when we needed to talk alone with visitors, but they could always knock and be received. In fact, my son Nathan grew quite adept at a kind of commando crawl and would sneak up on conversations, especially when voices dropped!

---

11 See glossary for more information.

The evening meal was something we did together, sitting around the table, away from the TV, to talk and listen to each other. This was our time of family communion. We tried joining with another family to have little worship meetings but this failed miserably, so while we always took the opportunity to pray when the need arose, it was these consistent mealtimes that brought us all together. I was confronted by the boys if I was absent in mind. They often mimicked me and my attempts to become involved in the family exchange of news, particularly if I noticed things months later than the rest of the household. We also realised that people had begun to notice that this time of the evening was when we were all at home, as this was when we received the most phone calls. So we instituted a 'not available at the moment and will call you back' policy at mealtimes. The local neighbourhood police officer became involved with us, and he would choose to pop round at mealtimes. Months later, he was talking about the extension he had added to his house. He told us that, having seen our family gather at mealtimes, he realised that was something he wanted for his own home – and as there was nowhere for a dining table, he had built an extension for this purpose. I suppose this was a little family witness.

Hospitality is hard to describe, but I think it is more apparent in the results, the feeling that the recipient is left with. When people come into our sphere, cross the threshold of our lives, do they feel attended to? Do they feel part – or segregated? Is there generosity of resources and time? Dawn plays a key role in this: it is she who makes the house a springboard for hospitality, and from an early age the boys also took part. One of the practical ways in which they did this was in making their rooms available – they would generally take turns to give up their room for guests, and would sleep elsewhere, the exception being if there were particular study periods and exams. I don't remember any protest, as they saw this as 'one of the things you do', and we as a family have been richly blessed by sharing 'down time' with different people passing through.

I have always wanted to make sure that we feed people well. When Dawn and I were travelling in the UK in the early days, we found that food was either feast or famine. People have different patterns of eating and we always try to fit with them. One household we stayed with ate very meagre meals. But they were into pickling their own onions, and they were very keen that we tried these. Well, with nothing else to be had we tucked in – I have never eaten so many pickled onions in my life! These experiences made me aware that travelling can leave different people hungry at different times, and I think it's the role of the host to make sure their guests are comfortable.

There was one dear brother who asked me to disciple him, and over a period of a year, he became very close with the family. He was energetic, but would sometimes suffer with a 'sugar drop', the result of which was to make him look floppy and miserable. On one occasion when my youngest, Jamie, was little, this chap was in a bad way. This time it was not food related but Jamie read the signs as well as he could at the time, and appeared at his side with a Mars Bar taken from his own selection box. Of course it was not the solution that was needed, but it said more to that brother about the care and hospitality that this little boy was communicating than any sumptuous meal or prayer ministry.

Making sure that I am living that which I believe has stayed very central to how I have sought to build. Putting things right with Dawn and the kids has to take priority. On one occasion I arrived at a meeting having had an argument with Dawn that was not resolved when I left home. I realised that I just couldn't stay, so I made my apologies and returned home to sort things out (Matt. 5:23–24). It is detrimental to your family, and I would say to the church as a whole, if your presented image doesn't ring true with what people know behind closed doors.

In London we have hosted a number of international conferences. Just as the church has gone on holiday together as a way of expressing relationship with each other, we have also hosted international delegates in our own homes. These conferences take some work to put on – preparing the programme, arranging visas and so on. However, universally the thing that is most spoken about and appreciated is the hospitality that each delegate experiences. It is this that other network members most want to achieve when we visit them. This seems to reinforce the thought that it is what we do that has the most impact, over and above what we say and what we believe.

III
Drinking at Many Streams

'John, as you know, I feel called to education and I believe that God has given me this role at this school. Jane and I are keen to be part of the church – it's just that I won't be able to attend all the church meetings.'

We are all to have an active role as followers of Jesus, within the community of believers and outside it in the 'world'. We also all have direct access to God – we can hear Him for ourselves! We are no longer dependent on someone else – a priest – to hear God for us.

The lesson of Bob

Bob was an imposing figure with a voice that could command the crew of a battleship in the midst of a bombardment. This sergeant major characteristic had no doubt been developed as he worked his way through key teaching positions in some of the most challenging schools in the country. Thus he was the last person you would expect to approach you with an air of apology, yet here he was on my front doorstep, with metaphorical cap in hand. The way he looked at me was more in line with a doffed-cap gardener talking to his duke than brothers speaking together.

Bob was not a new Christian – in fact he had been a member of a number of churches as he and his wife moved around the country – and he was to be a pioneer for us. It was 1983 and he had just been appointed to a failing school in east London as its head teacher. This was in the days before Ofsted, but it was clear that the school was in dire straits as Bob took it on, making what was to happen over the next ten years all the more remarkable. Rather apologetically he began, 'John, as you know, I feel called to education and I believe that God has given me this role at this school. Jane and I are keen to be part of the church – it's just that I won't be able to attend all the church meetings.'

To cut a long story short, this was not a problem to us. Bob's ministry was to that school and to education. We made sure there was a way in which he could feed back to us on his ministry and, although I am not one for 'spiritual warfare' which focuses on the 'spirit' of an area and the idea that a place needs to be exorcised, Bob would have the other leaders and me marching around the school grounds on a wet Saturday morning praying fervently for that school. In due course the school moved from being one of the worst in the country to one of the best, and this is the legacy that Bob gave to it and to the thousands of students who have passed through it to this day.

Bob was just one example of someone who was 'sent out' from us.[12] We decided not to restrict the role of church to some 'spiritual' meetings, but instead we recognised that our mission as believers is to affect the world: some are called to minister to the 'body' and some to minister in the marketplace – and many to do both.

Priesthood of all believers

We firmly believe in the priesthood of all believers – that is, that everyone has a priestly ministry. This doesn't mean we don't believe in spiritual authority or a church leadership team. But there is no group of professional ministers who are the 'doers' of spiritual activity while the rest are the 'done to'. We are all equipped to serve and minister. Of course, serving and ministry are pretty much the same thing: we minister to each other, we serve each other and we are ministers to the world as well.[13]

There are two things to look at here – two lessons or topics. The first is that we are to have an active role as followers of Jesus, within the community of believers and outside it in the 'world'. In this, all of us are ministers, not just those who hold roles of responsibility within the church community – all of us. Whether our primary time and effort is spent at home, in a church organisation, at school or in another workplace, this is all 'ministry'. We can look to God to equip us for all of life – we hold all as sacred before God. In that sense it is our ministry, our spiritual service[14].

---

12 In fact he also had significant input, with others from LifeLine Church, into Zambia and Uganda.

13 This is not to say we don't believe in paid church workers, but ministry is not restricted to them. We very much believe in investing in people.

14 'Therefore, I urge you, brothers and sisters, in view of God's mercy, to offer your bodies as a living sacrifice, holy and pleasing to God – this is your true and proper worship.' (Rom. 12:1)

We choose to see people as agents of change, affecting the world and those around. They are not empty vessels, but channels for God to work through.

In Isaiah 61 there is a proclamation: 'I am anointed to preach good news…' and so on – but as the passage goes on, those who have been doing the 'hearing' become the agents, the 'oaks of righteousness' who rebuild the broken places and become a blessing. We see this same sentiment in Ephesians 4 with the different ministries: apostle, prophet, evangelist, pastor, teacher. They are all to be present in the church, not for the sake of their ministry but to build the church up, to enable the people themselves to evangelise, prophesy etc. All believers should have a priestly mission; it is not reserved for the few. There should be team – this is not a role merely for professionals.

In Genesis 2:15 we see that 'The LORD God took the man and put him in the Garden of Eden to <u>work</u> it and take care of it' (emphasis added). Work was part of Adam's riches and his fellowship with his maker, not a consequence of the fall. God works and so do we. When God made us in His image, work was part of what He created for our existence. Work is part of our humanness and was intended to be part of God's creation, thereby bringing Him glory. So our lives – all our lives – are Christ's: our homes, our jobs, our money (tithing and offerings are only a minor part of what we do) – our whole life, surrendered and available, is offered to God in response to His love for us.

The second point is about the status we have. I have always been keen not to stand between another believer and God. The moment someone says, 'I think this is what God is leading me to do', the discussion is pretty much over, unless of course what they are doing is contrary to scripture. You see, I never want to put on the robes of the high priests of the Old Testament, who stood between the people and God. That's a pretty risky position, which is why they attached a rope to the priest's feet when he went behind the curtain into the Holy of Holies in the temple, just in case the sacrifice was unacceptable and God finished him off. When Jesus was crucified, the curtain or veil in the temple was torn in two (Matt. 27:51): no longer was there any barrier between the people and God. We can approach God ourselves: there is no special priesthood – we are all a nation of priests, a royal priesthood (1 Peter 2:9).

I would therefore not want to do anything to get in the way of people's direct access to God. And if they can have direct access to God, they can minister, just as I can as the church leader. In fact, I believe we should give room for all to minister. Does that mean we have a stream of people preaching on a Sunday morning? Well, we do have quite a rich variety, but not because it is an 'open mic' opportunity; we also need to recognise ministry and gift. Not everyone is gifted to preach or teach; some serve in that way, but there are other acts of service and ministry that we need to give room to in the body of Christ. We always try to give space for serving opportunities, and with those like Bob, whose ministry is not in the sight of the rest of us, we take the opportunity to hear, join with and pray. We show interest in each other, as what we are all doing is part of the ministry of this body of believers.

One of the most striking experiences of allowing people to minster to us was when we sent a team to Zimbabwe in the late 1990s. To us, the cities and towns looked impoverished: inflation was on the rise and all of us westerners, as we converted our pounds and dollars to the local currency, found we were millionaires. But when we went into the rural areas the poverty was even more apparent. In a rural district of Matabeleland the team had been teaching and ministering at schools and to the local churches. One evening towards the end of the first week, in the tent meeting, there came the time for the offering – but this offering was to be for us. Firstly, we were taken aback by the way people sprang from their seats and danced, sang and clapped their way to the offering pots. There was a particular old lady, with the broadest grin on her toothless face, dancing her way to the front with her hand clasping three copper coins. People were giving out of their lack, but joyfully. It seemed perverse for us to take this gift. After 200 people had given their offering, the total amounted to less than $20. What were we to do? We could not give it back: we had to allow these people to minister to us – after all, 'Whoever welcomes a prophet as a prophet will receive a prophet's reward, and whoever welcomes a righteous person as a righteous person will receive a righteous person's reward' (Matt. 10:41). However, this experience spoke to us, coming from our rich countries, about giving in abundance – we were ministered to. In the end I think we bought some cold drinks: it was truly a holy communion that we shared with each other. It was as though we could taste the sacrifice in the gift, and it was a special and humbling experience.

The heart of the house

It is important that whoever becomes part of the community comes with humility and adopts the heart of the house. In that sense, the humble way in which Bob came to me was indicative of an understanding of this house. We are known as a place of relationship and commitment, but that is bound in an almost unspoken way with a core practice and 'default' of serving. It would be easy for someone like Bob just to use our church merely as a base – after all, his ministry was to happen elsewhere. However, he and his wife joined with many of LifeLine's activities and teams. On one particularly tough trip to Dominica, Bob was part of a team with some female members who found themselves in some pretty shady accommodation. The team was disquieted and the women, who were mostly young and single, were unsettled about the security of their room which was some way away from the rest of the team. With no concern for his own comfort and before any other solution was proposed, Bob grabbed a blanket and pillow and, closing the girls in their room, slept in the corridor across their door. It was a very different position from that which one of the most successful educationalists in the UK might expect, but his ministry was to serve.

Valentines High School was to become a 'Beacon' school. It remains oversubscribed to this day, with people moving to the area to get their children into its catchment. It has been held up as an example and there is a steady trickle of teachers and educational leaders coming to learn from what has been done at Valentines and how the school has become such a success story.

'As we looked at what had happened over several years, we realised the benefit of being able to 'drink at several streams'. We had received the fruit from any number of ministries; we had not been restricted to one stream. In this way we had avoided the danger of demarcation that I call denominationalism…'

God is consistent but His message or direction alters at different times; the prophetic is therefore important, but it must also be weighed.

A different way to build

Our purpose is to love God, which is shown through obedience to the Lordship of Christ. If we are to truly love God, that has to translate into love of the brethren, which in turn is demonstrated through serving and fellowship.

When the church first started we were looking to one apostolic ministry[15] for oversight. In the course of things there was a leader sent to us who was a difficult character. He was gifted, but his manner was universally accepted to be trying. Other network leaders would say to me, 'How do you cope with him?' My answer was simple: 'I am called to serve in this way, and I have been equipped to love him – not necessarily to like his way of being'. However, this never got in the way of me confronting him: this love was empowering, not weakening.

If we are to obey God, we need to know what He is saying. In scripture, we have 'universal truth', the unchanging word of God. This is our bedrock and what we test all against, but there is also what I call the 'now word of God'. This is the particular emphasis or direction that God gives. We need to know the times and seasons of God. Jesus cursed a tree (Mark 11:12–25) because it was not giving fruit; it was not the season in the natural world for that tree to produce fruit, but he was looking to the tree for fruit and therefore it was out of step with him. We don't want be out of step with Christ. We want to be like the sons of Issachar (1 Chron. 12:32) who knew the times and seasons. As we see with God's people in the Bible, God is consistent but His message or direction alters at different times. Sometimes the people were encouraged to leave captivity, as with Moses, but sometimes they were led to support their masters: the stories of Joseph and

---

15 See glossary for more information.

Daniel demonstrate this. At other times they are told to wait and settle in captivity, as seen in Jeremiah. The 'now word of God' is important to grasp. As Arthur Wallis[16] would say, 'We need to know God's mind and His moment'.

Therefore, we are attentive to the prophetic. This is one of the primary ways we have determined our direction as a church. We are keen never to move into a structural or organisational approach that gets focused on the maintenance of a programme or a liturgical calendar, with the institution becoming more important than the people and a relational approach. Prophetic over programme is our way.

The Bible tells us to 'weigh' the prophetic (1 Cor. 14:29), so this is what we do. The leaders come together and consider the word: do we sense this is what God is bringing to us, and are there adjustments to be made? Is it in line with what God says in His word, and with the word of God given to us by His Spirit? We don't automatically accept or reject, because 'we have the mind of Christ' (1 Cor. 2:16; emphasis added). This means not just me as the senior leader, but all of our leadership team together.

Again, there are two ideas that we hold in tension.

> *So then, my beloved, just as you have always obeyed, not as in my presence only, but now much more in my absence, work out your salvation with fear and trembling.*
>
> — **Phil. 2:12, NASB** (emphasis added)

All believers have this responsibility to 'work out' their own faith. Primarily my role as a leader is to see people equipped and released into their own 'ministry' or their life in God. I don't want to get in the way of that – and I don't want to tell them what it is; I am merely there to add guidance, to teach well and highlight biblical principles. We together, after all, are the body of Christ.

On the other hand, I have a responsibility as shepherd to care for the flock and to protect. For example, one of the ways in which we have had to do this is to protect people's generosity: when it comes to offerings, we don't cajole or 'hype things up', as people are so ready to give.

---

16 Arthur Wallis was one of the most significant men who helped establish the house church movement – a great fount of wisdom and teaching.

Not everything has worked. It seemed good at one point to see if we could be more organised in how we went about serving. Someone devised a scheme called 'Available to serve', whereby each person would state their skills and when they were available to be called on. One cheeky church member latched onto this and was part-way through getting a house (purchased as an investment) renovated and redecorated free of charge and ready for resale before we realised the abuse. Hence, relationship needs not to be squeezed out by organisation and structure.

We continue to take direction from the prophetic. In recent times I have been asking God for what is next, and heard a clear calling for a 'spirit of adventure'. So that has directed our teaching and our tone.

When we started out, the church was really an amalgamation of different house groups, which were linked to a particular apostolic ministry. This was where we got our direction and oversight, but there came a time when they were directing us to go in a direction that we did not feel was right and there was a painful parting of ways.

Our heart was always to be joined, so we were rocked by this, and there were some key people at that time who reached out to us and sought to care for us and the church. A number of years later, Keith Hazell was visiting us. Keith was a prophet and had brought a number of important words to us. On this occasion he laid out a choice: 'You should either be something or join something!' adding, 'And I know what I think'. It was a pertinent challenge: we had walked with a metaphorical limp since the break with the original apostolic network, and here God was giving us a choice. As we looked at what had happened over several years, we realised the benefit of being able to 'drink at several streams'. We had received the fruit from any number of ministries; we had not been restricted to one stream. In this way we had avoided the danger of demarcation that I call denominationalism, where there is an assumption that all truth, and the perfect outworking of that truth, can be found only in this one setting and stream of churches.

The prophetic has often come to us at moments when we have had to make important directional decisions. The leaders had gathered away for a retreat, and there was a clear message about 'pouring out the oil'. This led to us deciding to invest in relationships and ministry abroad in places where there could be no expectation that costs would be covered. To give with an open hand has been grafted into our DNA. This word, combined with another which was about 'sowing your sons as seeds in foreign soil', I believe has borne great fruit as we have seen a closeness of relationship grow overseas – so that I might truly say I have planted sons in foreign soil.

Another directional word was about resources. A group of prophets had gathered in California and, as they prayed for me, they started speaking about a release of resource, which would be beyond what I had imagined. Now, I was a stockbroker of 18 years, so I have come across those with a lot of money. But as we started to get involved in our local community with the delivery of services through LifeLine Community Projects, the sense to 'go for growth' that I had received from these prophets spurred us on while circumstances would have said otherwise. We have never been very focused on numbers – what is in the bank account or numbers attending on a Sunday morning. However, we recently had cause to add up the money that has passed through just LifeLine Projects[17] (not the church or LifeLine Network International), and we were amazed to see that in excess of £50 million[18] had come to us. It has been a challenging and humbling experience to serve the wider community by deploying these resources. I never would have predicted this when the prophets spoke all those years ago.

Some of the input we have had has affected our 'flavour' as a church and as a network. To give one example of this, the ongoing relationship we have had with Mark McGrath for over 30 years has resulted in us being able to review and clearly express a gospel message focused on the Lordship of Christ.[19]

All this led to another important choice of 'people over plant'. We have chosen to invest in people and ministry over buildings and other assets. The lion's share of our expenditure is on people rather than 'stuff'. This will remain the case, as it is how we feel God has guided

---

17 See glossary for more information.

18 This figure relates to grants and contracts that we have administered and directed for the benefit of the communities we serve both in East London and abroad.

19 McGrath, M. with Russo, P. (2008). *A Forgotten Gospel*. Marietta, GA: Fields Pond Publishing.

us. The new chapter is around buildings: we now have some property which we will be developing, but we have been able to do this in such a way that it does not come with the need for a whole-church focus on a building fund. We want to remain focused on our affection and being good 'witnesses' beyond the walls of any building – we have striven too hard to become institutionalised now in our outlook or practice.

God has sometimes used our limited sight to get us into the right place within His purposes, when a more 'sighted' group of believers might have predicted what was to come and counted the cost more carefully.

God never intended for believers to be siphoned off from society – isolated in our churches. He meant us to make an impact on the world and influence political systems! Followers of Jesus, as they catch this truth, can often make better use of public funds – not to proselytise but to deliver services and provide solutions that serve the communities we live in and maximise public resources.

Kingdom without borders

'It's just little old us!' Do you ever find yourself saying this, or thinking it? It's a pretty dangerous thought pattern. We had years of consistent words coming to individuals and to the church as a whole, extolling our significant place and role, recognising what God had planted in us. We would even teach on significance, but there was a nagging sense of smallness and unbelief. If the statement, 'What good has ever come from Nazareth?' (John 1:46) was said about Jesus, we definitely took on the same for ourselves: 'What good has ever come out of Dagenham?' In our thinking, we were post-industrial like our locality: we had a foreboding feeling that our best days had passed us by and we were part of a declining story.

The result of this was the 'ten-foot hatpin'[20]. When commended by others, when people seemed impressed with what God was doing among us, we would shuffle our feet, try to crack a joke and move on, denying in our hearts what had just been said. We were the essence of the under-stated: there was never a whiff of hype, or much expressed excitement. Now, let me come clean. This has a lot to do with me: I have not been blessed with an expressive face, and this is exacerbated by a somewhat reticent approach to verbal and facial expression (hence Daniel and I writing this together). So how I am, has I think, affected us corporately – and you should see the blank faces before me as I preach on a Sunday morning!

---

20 For younger readers – we don't see hatpins very often nowadays, but in the past they were somewhat dangerous pins used to fix a hat to the head (or rather the hair) of the wearer. They were not small, but they were not ten feet long. The idea here is that if anything got inflated we would rapidly bring it down to size, hence the over-the-top sized hatpin.

The ten-foot hatpin would come into play the moment that anything seemed to inflate, anytime we thought we were 'a bit good' or there was something special or, worse still, if anyone seemed a little too big for their boots. Sometimes there was a not-very-nice characteristic at play to do with bringing people down to size, but more frequently this was a self-inflicted mechanism for 'deflating' the stories we shared with each other, how we talked about what God was doing in our lives, what successes we were seeing. It was as though as soon as we started to hear something good about ourselves, we had the urge to grab a huge hatpin and puncture a hole in what we were hearing. It thus often took a third party to accurately describe our impact, both corporately and individually.

Not so long ago the church was hosting an international conference and the delegates took it upon themselves to commend the leaders and my ministry back to the church. This was not something we had orchestrated, and certainly not something we had planned for. It was an honest act of thanksgiving and testimony, and on the face of it we really couldn't explain it. Daniel had invited along a sister who was in another church but shared the vision of LifeLine, who had walked alongside us with the various expressions of that vision over quite a period of time. While we were feeling quite awkward at the actions of the delegates and wanting to make sure we 'could get on with the programme', Daniel spotted her, quite overcome with what was happening, a tear running down her face. She was more in tune with the rightness of what was going on, and the declarations that were being made about us, than we were ourselves. It was a prompting to put away those hatpins, to recognise God's work among us – that it is good and marvellous in our sight! (Ps. 118)

On the other hand, God has sometimes used our limited sight to get us into the right place within His purposes, when a more 'sighted' group of believers might have predicted what was to come and counted the cost more carefully. If you feel you have just a bit-part to play, you don't necessarily consider the whole piece, the grandness of the vision, its complexities and challenges; you are much more likely just to get on with your bit, head down and confident in your 'small part'. This was certainly the case in our involvement both in Sierra Leone and in Barking and Dagenham.

'Ridiculous hope'

Jamie coined this phrase a few years ago. By that time, we realised that we were often operating with a 'ridiculous hope': that is, a vision or expectation which seems improbable and unlikely, a kind of 'the blind see and the lame walk' (Isa. 35:5–6, Matt. 11:5) anticipation. Hope, of course, is dangerous: it is easier to be resigned to the present situation – it is easier not to hope – because if things do not change for the better we can feel hurt and betrayed by our own emotions. 'Ridiculous hope' is a stage further on: if hope is not a cert, to have ridiculous hope of positive change is close to madness. But we found that we were starting to view the situation God was putting us into with a righteous ambition that was out of character with our humble beginnings and under-stated manner. The ten-foot hatpin had been well and truly packed away.

In 1990 I met the late Richard Cole in Shrewsbury, Shropshire, in a series of circumstances that I now recognise were God-breathed. He brought us together; I won't go into all of it now, but this was one of those strange occurrences when your heart is knitted with someone else's by God. Without us knowing each other, we were brothers in a way I had never experienced before. I walked into the room where he was sitting and both of us knew that we were preordained to meet and relate. It is the one time I have experienced 'love at first sight' – although it would be better to call it *agape* at first sight'. Little did we know how that meeting would affect the rest of our lives, and how soon our meeting and connection would be tested by real circumstances. It would not be flippant to say that Richard Cole was someone whose faith was tested by fire. Many times that was gunfire.

Soon after this meeting he was back in west Africa, and as the war in Liberia triggered a conflict and civil war in Sierra Leone, Richard was in the middle of things – with some remarkable stories of God's protection. Guns did not fire when held to his head; a church was hidden in a flat and preserved while there was slaughter all around; he had a short period as an honorary major with a detachment of troops following him around.

Boy soldiers

The legitimate government of Sierra Leone asked Richard if he could do anything with the former combatants, boy soldiers, who had been with the rebels. He came to me and asked whether, if he was to do this, we would be in it with him. I want you to understand this was not about an African organisation seeking a British sponsor; he wanted co-ownership, even to the extent that the funding would come into the project via LifeLine Network International. This was to be *our* inheritance: not his, not mine, but ours together. We determined together, Richard and I, to pioneer a new approach, to operate in partnership – including finance – and see God's power and provision together. In the UK we saw the provision as coming from God rather than being the provision ourselves. This meant that on the occasions when we had to call Richard to say that the bank account was empty, and there was no money for food, he would reply, 'When the bank is red, we say hallelujah'. It meant we were thrown back on God being the provider – and it was as we put the phone down that there would be a miraculous offer of a donation.

In pretty short order we found ourselves co-labouring. The vision was not focused merely on rescue, but on rebuilding. Our shared vision was that these boys who had been taken for evil purposes and engaged in evil things[21] would be those who would rebuild Sierra Leone – a generation of leaders.

As the focus was rebuilding, not merely escape, we called the work the Nehemiah Project. The book of Nehemiah speaks of a young man who returns to Jerusalem to rebuild its walls. We read this as a prophetic statement of the very thing we wanted to see. Our faith is one of empowerment, so when we look at powerful proclamations like the one in Isaiah 61, we see two distinct roles. The first is our part, as followers 'anointed to…' Here the speaker is talking about 'me':

---

21 BBC reporter Jeremy Vine featured the Nehemiah Project. He interviewed Civilian, a former child soldier, and Richard Cole for 'From Our Own Correspondent'. This feature won the Amnesty International Radio Award in June 2000.
See 'From Our Own Correspondent: Children – weapons of war', BBC News website, 13 April 1999.

> *The Spirit of the Sovereign* LORD *is on me,*
>   *because the Lord has anointed me*
>   *to proclaim good news to the poor.*
> *He has sent me to bind up the broken-hearted,*
>   *to proclaim freedom for the captives*
>   *and release from darkness for the prisoners,*
> *to proclaim the year of the Lord's favour*
>   *and the day of vengeance of our God,*
> *to comfort all who mourn,*
>   *and provide for those who grieve in Zion –*
> *to bestow on them a crown of beauty*
>   *instead of ashes,*
> *the oil of joy*
>   *instead of mourning,*
> *and a garment of praise*
>   *instead of a spirit of despair.*
>
> — Isa. 61:1–3

But the second role appears part-way through verse 3, and here the focus is 'they':

> *They will be called oaks of righteousness, a planting of the Lord*
>   *for the display of his splendour.*
>
> *They will rebuild the ancient ruins*
>   *and restore the places long devastated;*
> *they will renew the ruined cities*
>   *that have been devastated for generations.*
>
> — Isa. 61:3–4

All of this second section is about what will be done by those who hear the good news – those who were the broken-hearted, the captives. They are not sitting to one side having ministry 'done to' them; they are part of the next wave: 'they will renew the ruined cities'. This was our 'ridiculous hope' for the conflict, for the scarred young people who became part of the Nehemiah Project. They were to become a solution where it was least expected: those who had been purposed and perverted for destruction were to be a 'planting of the Lord'.

The story of Richard Cole and the boys of the Nehemiah Project is worthy of a book of its own – and a couple of films! So rather than recounting those details here, let us just look at the starkest contrasts in their story.

As the civil war ravaged Sierra Leone, boy soldiers were often at the forefront of the destruction. They did not have the inhibitions of adults – they had been effectively brainwashed, and showed little fear and seemingly little remorse for their actions. So understandably, when they were captured or turned themselves in to government and peace-keeping forces, their home communities did not want them back. Part of the technique employed by the rebel leaders was to have the boys attack their own communities and families, thereby destroying any sense of loyalty to or connection with the community. The rebel group became their only place of belonging.

Fast forward to 2014 and the Ebola outbreak in west Africa. This was a terrible enemy that attacked without warning and did not allow for the sick to be cared for by their loved ones, for fear of spreading the disease. The result for those children who had survived Ebola while the rest of their family perished was that they were ostracised by their communities: nobody wanted them near. What few familiar faces survived were turned away from them. But all was not lost, because the Nehemiah boys, now young men, were ideally placed with their families to respond to these new 'conflict' orphans – orphans just as they had been. What's more, they were at the forefront of delivering food to those in quarantine and in the communities that had rejected them. They became the 'rebuilders' of broken places, and a focal point for restoration.

'SERVING THE COMMUNITY AT THE EXPENSE OF THE COMMUNITY'

Richard was very clear from the start that doing this work and serving the nation would not be funded merely by church donations. The conflict in Sierra Leone was not a problem of the church; it was a problem born of the wider community, and the wider community – local, national and international – would pay for the good work that we would do together. There can be no question of his level of commitment: he still had 'skin in the game'. The induction process for any new boy demonstrates this.

Each new boy was taken into Richard's home, and would live with his family for two weeks. The boys needed to learn to be in community and in family, after the survival of the jungle life that they had lived. They had to be taught co-dependence to counter their previous unchecked, feral existence. The best place for them to learn this was in a place where they would be loved. The message that we were learning and seeking to put across was that the followers of Jesus could make better use of public funds – delivering services, providing solutions – than could be done by others. Our faith was what drove us to new heights.

As we, back in London, saw what Richard was doing and aided him by pursuing UK-based funding, the phrase 'serving the community, in the needs of the community, at the expense of the community'[22] started to turn over and over in our minds. Was there some way to pursue that vision here? Was there something we in the UK could learn from Sierra Leone?

As a result of the various conflicts in the former Yugoslavia and the post-Soviet era in eastern Europe, combined with African and Asian immigration in the late 1990s, east London in general and Dagenham in particular was receiving a large number of immigrants and asylum seekers. Large quantities of social and 'right-to-buy' housing meant that this part of London was one of the few places where 'newly arrived' professional families could get on the housing ladder. When people claimed asylum, the government sent large numbers to councils that had housing stock. This phenomenon, combined with low levels of education in this post-industrial setting where many had low aspirations, resulted in one of the most deprived local areas in the UK. There was a clear need, and it was a case of us needing to decide what was 'ours' to do.

---

22 This was a prophetic word which we took on as a church and network.

A number of organisations and projects we have started can be rooted back to this key time: LifeLine Community Projects, the FaithAction network, Community Resources[23], SW!TCH ID and Peaced Together[24] – but what is important is to get to grips with the catalysts for these, and the turning points.

As in the church base in London, within LifeLine Network International it is relationship between the network members, not a doctrinal agreement, that is the key thing holding us together. We don't seek to operate a 'hub and spoke' model; we don't want a religious imperialism, where everything is expected to flow 'from the west to the rest'. That's why we are forever keen to learn from and share with each other. One evening I was stirred by a picture that came to me of wealth and waste. I saw money sloshing around, but being wasted: no value was being added to this wealth. This was a turning point for us, as it made us look at the resources – in the shape of government and European Community funding – coming into east London.

By now we had worked with Richard Cole for a number of years in Sierra Leone and seen the Nehemiah Project take shape. There was another significant scripture for this period: the riches of the wicked shall come to the righteous (Prov. 13:22)[25]. We got a sense not only that we *could* take part in the community around us, but that we were *supposed* to – it was our right and duty. We started talking about 'impacting individuals' and 'influencing systems'.

The local voluntary sector needed an overhaul: too many were content to moan at the state of affairs, but not to partner in seeking resolution and change. When we started operating, we came with a solution-focused mentality, for which we are now known; it was probably born a little out of ignorance, and certainly innocence. We found that this attitude was at odds with that of the local voluntary sector, and too often that of church organisations as well. The resigned, whingeing modus operandi was stifling – but this was the place we were given to.

---

23 See glossary for more information.

24 See glossary for more information.

25 See also these translations of Prov. 13:22:
'A good life gets passed on to the grandchildren; ill-gotten wealth ends up with good people.' (MSG)
'But the wealth of the wicked is reserved for the righteous.' (ISV)

So we prayed and listened for what God would have us do. This meant that at one point, when all the local players were united against us (we were barred from meetings, voted off committees, etc.), God clearly said not to defend ourselves but to 'stand firm, and see the salvation of the LORD' (Ex. 14:13, ESV). Not only did they fail in their attempts to destroy us, but we shot up from being a Dagenham-focused training provider to being regional – across London – and national. In fact, within a year, those organisations that had striven to cut us off were receiving funding through us and sub-contracting from us as well.

We found, again and again, that God's word came to us, from visiting ministries and from a study we did as a church on the books of 1 and 2 Kings. As we started reaching out to those without English language in our local community, a former imam, Mohammad, became connected to us.

Mohammad's philosophy was simple: 'Show them the Kingdom and they will find the King.' Now, I would not want to deny the importance of declaring the gospel but, as a way of helping get over some evangelical barriers, Mohammad's phrase was very helpful: it allowed us to recalibrate. You see, our primary task is to show what God is like and to love each other. One of our leaders said one day, 'I finally feel that I don't have to view my neighbours as targets. I can love them as friends, and it's up to the Holy Spirit what happens next.' It does sound biblical – we are not called to make converts, after all: Matthew 28:19 says 'go and make <u>disciples</u>…' (emphasis added).

We started to see the work of LifeLine Projects as a sort of church plant. We weren't necessarily in a different area, trying to recreate a new, smaller version of ourselves; no, we were in the same area, but touching the lives of people we had never been able to connect with before, namely those from different faith backgrounds. This was part of the journey of a *church without walls*: first and foremost valuing relationship over religion and meetings; an international network of relationships; called to operate in the world, as Bob had demonstrated; and called now to work in the local community, corporately and as individuals.

As we grew and became more established in our publicly funded training provision, other churches and faith groups started to seek our advice and to learn from our journey. This resulted in due course with the launching of FaithAction, which is a network of faith-based organisations serving their local communities. The FaithAction team, originally drawn from LifeLine, was soon offering advice to organisations throughout the UK, and representing and advocating for faith-based organisations to government.

We cannot afford to have a 'little old us' mentality, as it causes us to miss what we are purposed for. Our work all started when our hearts were captured by the vision of rebuilding a whole nation on the west coast of Africa. This was best reflected back to us by a Sierra Leonean who was part of Richard Cole's church many years ago: 'LifeLine is so precious to me, as you have held my nation in your heart when no one else did…'

We want to remain like watchmen on the walls, alert to God's activity, never thinking that we have all truth 'nailed down', but neither wanting to be chasing fads and novelty. We don't want to miss out on what God is doing, and we remain keen to be used by Him.

If we are to be an accurate reflection of God, to show what He is like, we have to have a heart for more than just our own little thing.

We can choose to have 'church as a field', whereby all activity and cultivation happens in the field, and everyone must come to the field – that is, the activities of the church organisation.

OR

We can choose to have 'church as a force': smashing down the walls of church, being uncontainable in our attitudes and mission, affecting the world around us.

Apostolic community

The very nature of an apostolic community[26] is to be sending and giving: '…and you will be my witnesses in Jerusalem, and in all Judea and Samaria, and to the ends of the earth.' (Acts 1:8). You have to be outward looking to achieve this. You have to have a heart for God's world. If we are to be an accurate reflection of God, to show what He is like, we have to have a heart for more than just our own little thing. Therefore, we have to be net exporters and net producers – we cannot be solely consumers. As a community of Christians, we don't expect to use up all we produce internally within our local church, whether this be finance, teaching or serving; we expect to make a significant contribution to things outside of us, both into the wider church and into the world.

'Don't get involved… Don't get contaminated… Don't get infected by this world!' As I grew up, these were the warnings, often unspoken, but hinted at pretty loudly. The attitude showed in things like the way we were taught to look at fashion, music, culture and university education: 'Why would you want to go to university?' The words were not always as clear as this, but the underlying theme was: keep away, protect yourself, and come quickly Jesus and rescue us before we slip into this overwhelming quicksand of sin and death! Of course, there are some elements of truth in these attitudes, but they seem a long way from the ideas of priestly sonship and princely inheritance that we see throughout the Bible. Let's look at what is said about our priestly position and the sonship that we inherit through Christ.

---

26 See glossary for more information.

The Resurrection Spirit Lives in Us

And if <u>the Spirit of him who raised Jesus</u> from the dead is living in you, he who raised Christ from the dead will also give life to your mortal bodies because of his Spirit who lives in you.

— Rom. 8:11 (emphasis added)

Co-heirs with Christ

Now if we are children, then we are heirs — heirs of God and <u>co-heirs with Christ</u>, if indeed we share in his sufferings in order that we may also share in his glory.

— Rom. 8:17 (emphasis added)

More than Conquerors

What, then, shall we say in response to these things? <u>If God is for us, who can be against us?</u> He who did not spare his own Son, but gave him up for us all — how will he not also, along with him, graciously give us all things? Who will bring any charge against those whom God has chosen? It is God who justifies. Who then is the one who condemns? No one. Christ Jesus who died — more than that, who was raised to life — is at the right hand of God and is also interceding for us. <u>Who shall separate us from the love of Christ?</u> Shall trouble or hardship or persecution or famine or nakedness or danger or sword? As it is written:

*"For your sake we face death all day long;
we are considered as sheep to be slaughtered."*

No, in all these things <u>we are more than conquerors</u> through him who loved us. For I am convinced that <u>neither death nor life</u>, neither angels nor demons, neither the present nor the future, nor any powers, <u>neither height nor depth</u>, <u>nor anything else in all creation</u>, will be able to separate us from the love of God that is in Christ Jesus our Lord.

— Rom. 8:31–39 (emphasis added)

Our inheritance cannot be just hanging on for heaven! We need to be living with the expectation and realisation of 'God/Christ-life' now. Thus we are not designed to be preserved in a kind of holy huddle, like a group of penguins shuffling together to avoid the perilous cold of worldliness. No! Instead we are to affect the world we are in. Some are called to work directly for the church, to be on the payroll; all of us are called to serve one another (the church), affect the good of 'the city' (Jer. 29:7) (in our community) and be witnesses of Christ, showing what God is like to those around us – wherever 'around us' may be. Incidentally, this affects the whole way we regard children. We love and nurture them, but we also recognise that they have a role in 'seeking the kingdom' (Matt. 6:33) and being influencers for God, 'arrows' (Ps. 127:4) of God's purpose in the places they are as well.

When I was growing up, if you were really 'spiritual' you were 'called' into full-time ministry. This might mean being a minister of a church, or a missionary. In many ways it was like the monastic calling of old. People were called out of 'the world' to be set apart, holy. Strange, is it not? To take monks, those most enthusiastic for God, and tuck them neatly away from the world where they could have only a limited impact on it? Let me be clear that I am not condemning this kind of life as a decision – it would be pretty hypocritical if I did, as a full-time minster myself. But the problem we faced then was that there were only two routes: a 'second-rate' route in 'the world', or a 'holy' route in the church.

It was not meant to be that way – we were never supposed to have a specialised, elite group of church workers. The fivefold Ephesians 4 ministries were not to be the preserve of a few. The role of the church leader, be it the evangelist, prophet, pastor or so on, is not to run around evangelising, prophesying or doing all the pastoring. No, the role is instead to release the people to minister – 'body ministry' is the ministry of the Body of Christ, and that means all of us!

I remember visiting a church for a baptism. It was a fairly vibrant crowd of able-bodied people, and there was a hearty time of singing lead by the pastor on a guitar. As the time for the baptism approached, he reached across and started a tape playing, while he smoothly jumped into a full rubber suit, covering his shirt, tie, jacket, trousers and all! He then nipped down into the baptistery, baptised each person on his own, and more or less raced the last one out of the pool so that he could take off the rubber suit, preach and lead the last song. It was quite something to watch, and quite entertaining for the congregation who happily looked on, thinking – one assumes – that they were getting good mileage out of their paid church worker. Entertaining – but surely unnecessary: what an opportunity for body ministry missed. All manner of actions performed by that pastor could have been done by others. In fact, what a joy it is to join in with baptism – to play a part and celebrate what we often call the 'happiest funeral ever'.[27]

The point to all of this is that the ministers should be all of us. As a leader in church I should be releasing that ministry in the body. That's why I don't like the term 'pastor': I am not the pastor, and there are many who take on a pastoring role. Do I care for people? Do I pastor? Of course, but I am not the pastor!

> *So Christ himself gave the apostles, the prophets, the evangelists, the pastors and teachers, to equip his people for works of service, so that the body of Christ may be built up…*
> — **Eph. 4:11–12** (emphasis added)

If I have the gift of evangelism, I must be looking to release others to be inspired and evangelise. If I have the gift of a pastor, then I am looking to release the congregation to care for one another.

The Ephesians 4 ministries are not a Christian career pinnacle, but a means to an end. The end is to equip the people, to build up; it is not about the minister being built up, but the church, the people as a whole. The way some speak, at times it would seem that the church is there to provide for the ministry of the apostle or leader, but that's the wrong way round. The apostle is there to serve the church, not vice versa.

If, as a leader, I am seeking to release people into ministry, I need to recognise that not all have been built the same: some will find their full expression in the confines of church life, but many will find that their primary point of 'Christ-life' is outside the meetings and gatherings of church, in the world – the school, playground, classroom, office and building site. God has made people like this.

We are supposed to be a force in the world. Jerry Cook puts this so well in *Love, Acceptance and Forgiveness*:[28] we can choose to have 'church as a field', whereby all activity and cultivation happens in the field,

---

27 We have produced a little booklet on baptism – if you would like to know more please contact us.

28 Cook, J. with Baldwin, S. (1979). *Love, Acceptance and Forgiveness: Equipping the Church to be Truly Christian in a Non-Christian World*. Ventura, CA: Regal Books.

and everyone must come to the field – that is, the activities of the church organisation. The whole thing becomes about a 'programme'. In some ways, it's about occupying people and entertaining them, and certainly about keeping folk out of trouble – a bit of a holy huddle. However, there is an alternative. Jerry Cook sets out the challenge of being 'church as a force': smashing down the walls of church, being uncontainable in our attitudes and mission, affecting the world around us; going to where people are poor and in need (the 'poor in spirit' [Matt 5:3]); not steering clear of the world but fully engaged, making a difference, leaving a mark.

> *'In the same way, let your good deeds shine out for all to see, so that everyone will praise your heavenly Father.*
>
> — **Matt. 5:16, NLT**

Integrity is not hard to understand theoretically: say it and do it; 'let your yes be yes and your no be no' (Matt. 5:37). The question is how we apply this when under pressure — that is when it is hard.

Legalism breeds hypocrisy and it is always riled by integrity.

Hearing it, saying it, doing it – integrity and faith

I do love a shortcut: I don't want to hang about or go the long way round. I think most people are the same, even though sometimes you do have to go the long way. However, because there is so often the desire to take the easy route, other people can create pressures on us to do less than the right thing.

Daniel was recently driving in Spain and trying to find his way back to his accommodation with a car full of tired kids and a family in another car following him. Everyone was tired and they were heading for traffic. In a moment of inspiration, or so he thought, he reset the sat nav for a shortcut and, gratifyingly, was guided off the motorway. He was led to turn first this way, then that; the sat nav was pretty definite about where he should go, but the road quality was deteriorating, until eventually he was directed to something that was a cross between a dirt track and a riverbed. It was at this point that he remembered that this was an English sat nav, not a Spanish one, and maybe it didn't have the most up-to-date maps. There were some queries raised by the other passengers, but the car behind was still following, so on he went. In fact, he was only on the dirt track for 100 metres when he came to a well-lit roundabout and a very substantial road. It would seem that the sat nav was prophetic and knew where the road was to be… or maybe that the Spanish road builders were behind schedule but had already submitted their plans, and the road was showing on the sat nav as complete. On this occasion it all worked out in the end – but it is never good to follow blindly, choosing to ignore your internal navigation and assuming that what another person has chosen to do (perhaps at the cost of integrity) will do for you.

It is integrity that I am most often asked to speak on when I am sharing overseas. When people have heard of our Doulos course they are most interested in integrity. When LifeLine Network International members have taken on the running of employment-related courses in Sierra Leone and Dominica, the thing that employers come back saying again and again is, 'We want LifeLine graduates because they display integrity'. We always look to deliver our teaching by incorporating practical and live scenarios, as the application is where things get interesting: it's all easy to do in theory in a classroom, but in life – well that's something else. Integrity is not hard to understand theoretically: say it and do it; let your yes be yes and your no be no (Matt. 5:37). The question is how we apply this when under pressure – that is when it is hard.

We have found that legalism and integrity have often collided. Legalism, at its core, is adding to the word of God: it's that case again of saying, 'Nice try Jesus, but I don't think you covered it all, so I'll add some more rules just to ensure my salvation.' The religious 'sat nav' tries to take us on a different route: aside from the gospel of faith and grace, other rules come up, traditions, expectations: don't rock the boat, don't upset people, just accept these additional rules. In many ways legalism makes things easier. For example, the Bible says not to get drunk; it doesn't say 'do not drink'. In fact, the Bible is often focused on excess generally. It's much simpler to say that you shouldn't drink at all – then, of course, you can't get drunk. But the Bible doesn't say that! Far be it from me to decide to impose my own rules above what guidance Jesus Himself gave! As above, I always want to be careful not to take up a position between someone else and God. I want to do all I can to facilitate their being closer with God; I don't want to throw up 'stumbling blocks' (Rom. 14:13-23) or false restrictions and rules.

It is in the position of church leader that I have had most challenge to integrity. I have always felt it so important to make sure our beliefs match our practice. Many years ago there was a group in the church who kept falling into gossip. The leaders had tried to address this, there had been meetings with individuals and with groups, but the thing kept popping up again and again. So we decided to take things to another level. I called them all together and announced that in three weeks we would be coming together to share the bread and wine, where we would look for the fullness of what is outlined in the Bible to come about.

> *For I received from the Lord what I also passed on to you: The Lord Jesus, on the night he was betrayed, took bread, and when he had given thanks, he broke it and said, "This is my body, which is for you; do this in remembrance of me." In the same way, after supper he took the cup, saying, "This cup is the new covenant in my blood; do this, whenever you drink it, in remembrance of me." For whenever you eat this bread and drink this cup, you proclaim the Lord's death until he comes.*
>
> *So then, whoever eats the bread or drinks the cup of the Lord in an unworthy manner will be guilty of sinning against the body and blood of the Lord. Everyone ought to examine themselves before they eat of the bread and drink from the cup. For those who eat and drink without discerning the body of Christ eat and drink judgment on themselves. That is why many among you are weak and sick, and a number of you have fallen asleep. But if we were more discerning with regard to ourselves, we would not come under such judgment. Nevertheless, when we are judged in this way by the Lord, we are being disciplined so that we will not be finally condemned with the world.*
>
> — 1 Cor. 11:23–32

Needless to say, there was much scurrying around as people sought to set things right with each other so that they would not be taking the cup in an 'unworthy manner'. However, there was one older man who decided that to get around all this, he would not turn up to the meeting. A few days after the meeting, out of the blue, he had a heart attack! He was taken to hospital and over the next period of time the medics tried to find the cause. Their conclusion was very revealing: they could find no cause of the heart attack, and nor could they find anything wrong, so they concluded it must be stress. This certainly sharpened how we view communion. We take the Bible very seriously as it affects our lives today.

On a number of occasions when we have been working with other churches or Christian organisations, there has been some requirement to sign non-smoking and teetotal pledges on behalf of the group (I have always found this disturbing – how can someone purport to sign a commitment about personal behaviour, and in response to a legalistic requirement at that, for anyone other than oneself?) I was required to sign such a pledge on behalf of all from LifeLine who would be serving on one particular project. When I questioned why and asked what it was about, I was accused of with 'compromising'. I set them straight, explaining that the far greater compromise would be to abandon a grace gospel and impose legalistic requirements on others. Another church leader spoke to me privately about the teetotal pledge. 'We all have to sign it in our denomination,' he said, 'but none of us keep to it – we just keep it quiet.' You see, my response went against the flow and started to unearth the hypocrisy operating behind the scenes. Legalism breeds hypocrisy and it is always riled by integrity.

So why write about these painful experiences? Well, strange as it may seem, many of these trials have actually become 'monument stones' – the acts of God in our lives, things that we have come through, growing in the process. We are on a pilgrimage, always learning and seeking to find God's purpose in all circumstances, not settling in bitterness, or for what we are comfortable with.

Attitude is always what is most important in the middle of painful experiences such as relationships that have gone wrong. We might not always get everything right but the condition of our heart is what's important. That is how we are called to be: Christ-like, forgiving 'seventy times seven' (Matt. 18:22). Not grasping for anything – even our own reputation.

The chapter we didn't want to write – Splits, division, leaving and soft-heartedness

Does it ever seem to you that the thing God calls you to is the thing you have to suffer over the most? We have certainly seen that when it comes to relationship. I don't know how we do it, but we don't seem to suffer around money or doctrine; we suffer over relationship – the very thing that God has called us to. In fact, we often joke that if God could call us to poverty the way He has called us to relationship, rather than suffering broken fellowship we could be struggling instead with great riches!

Leaving is an interesting thing – in so many ways it looks much like joining. If we picture one person leaving from a house and another arriving, both are acting in relation to the door: neither is in the house, and in fact they may have the same distance from it. They mirror each other's position: they look the same, but facing a different way. Yet the two experiences feel very different: joining is often initially an easy exercise, full of light conversation and lunch invitations, whereas leaving comes with a sense of distance and awkward conversations. I describe it as such because I don't want you to think leaving is easy. We have not cracked it, and I sometimes wonder how we can 'do' leaving better.

Let me point out that I am being deliberate with my choice of language: we are not talking about 'sending' here. Sending has generally been a more joyous experience, where we all together recognise God's calling for someone to go elsewhere – we have been able to change some leaving into sending, which is a good resolution. With the nature of communications and technology, sending does not need to be like leaving at all; and some are sent not to a different location but perhaps to a different sector, a call to minister in a workplace as much as in another city.

So why is leaving so different from joining? It's back to the picture of the people approaching and departing from the house – it's about the way they are facing. When you leave, your face is turned away, your vision elsewhere. Thus it is vision that can be the difference: do I see myself here? Pursuing this vision? Does this complement what is on my heart? Sadly, all too often people do leave churches without vision: there are push factors – they don't want to be there – but there is no pull factor of what and where they want to go to. There have been times when people have left to follow the fad of not meeting together, and ended up shipwrecked.

If vision is important, then surely the more visions the better? Wrong! More than one vision is 'di-vision'. Of course there can be different facets of vision and complementing parts, and we have certainly seen this to great effect. But vision is to do with direction, and if there are two different directions things can't work. Better to identify it swiftly and part company.

You can see here how individual leaving has a similar root to that of the church split (a corporate leaving). So many times we could have been saved pain if there had been an honest expression of separate vision, but people and leaders don't always know themselves what they want. We have seen many define themselves not by what they are, but by what they are not, or what they are no longer. It's odd, but there can often be little groups of people who are connected for no other reason than that they were previously part of the same thing – church, organisation or business – and now they are not. A mutuality of moaning.

One group that left us initially described themselves in a way that constantly referred back to the fact that they had been part of us but had left. Odd that they would want to define themselves by what they had left rather than what they were called to now. This soon changed and they started to reach a part of the community that we never had. Conversely, with the new freedom that we had to pursue what God had laid on our hearts, we were soon reaching people we had never been able to before: our work into the community took a new turn, as well as our overseas work, while they also maintained an overseas presence.

Net result: the Kingdom of God was expanded, both in terms of people and also in terms of our learning and shaping, our opportunity to forgive, and more.

Boy was it painful at the time – I wouldn't choose such a path – and yet, '…not my will but yours, Lord!' (Luke 22:42) After a period of attrition, when some we expected to go stayed, and some we thought would stay went, I said that we as a body would no longer discuss the presented issues with those who had gone; we were looking forward. I can honestly say we have never looked back: that split shaped us, not in a scarring, disabling way, but for the future. There is no doubt in my mind now that God used it for His purpose.

As regards mutualities of moaning – there's not much we can do when people have 'opted out' and formed an alliance of discontent. However, often these groups don't start once people have left: they have already started while the people are still part – or appear to be still part – of us.

We read in the Bible, again and again, to beware of talk. The tongue is a powerful and dangerous weapon. James describes it as like a rudder: something very small that can steer the whole ship into trouble (James 3:4). Once we get into negative talk and gossip, the polluting effects are great. Speaker and listener are equally affected. Things take on a political nature, rather than that of a loving family, and those previously without a problem are dragged into carrying phantom bullets, issues that they can hardly grasp but which result in them still managing to take offence.

So what can be done?

There's no room for gossip: that has to be identified and challenged and repented of. Gossip opens the door for the enemy to enter, and it's not just about false facts. But the fact is that there will always be leavers.

How should we be, in the midst of splits and leavings, since these are sadly all too common – 'went-ings' rather than 'sendings'? Our attitude is what is most important in the middle of it all – and we don't always get everything right. The best example I have observed has been a dear brother in New England who had a thriving church. He was hungry to move the church on: we came into relationship and started to minister there, while he started to minister throughout the LifeLine network. Then there came trouble with his elders, who did not want to move in this direction. Coupled with a spirit of individualism, this led to a church split.

During this period, this brother and his wife had made their home into a children's home. They were fostering and adopting children; he was speaking into local government about child policy, and modelling a different approach. A group from the church had stayed with him, and seemed to be part of this vision. However, it wasn't to be and, as things turned sour, the leaders sought to wrestle everything from him – including the assets of the charity that by this time owned the children's home – their home. The family was forced to move from New England to lodge with his wife's elderly father in another part of the US. But through all this time, never has he spoken a hateful word. He is an absolute picture of forgiveness and soft-heartedness. Now, I am not saying he is perfect or that he didn't make mistakes along the way, but the condition of his heart is second to none. That is how we are called to be: Christ-like, forgiving 'seventy times seven' (Matt. 18:22), not grasping for anything – even our own reputation.

There is something in the story of the young men from Israel told in Daniel. They are called to do the unrighteous thing and bow down to the king and worship him. They refuse to do this, and are faced with a fiery ordeal. They enter the furnace with faith and expectation, but say they will not change even if God does not rescue them. The king relents and has them pulled out: he has seen an angel walking with them.

> *So Shadrach, Meshach and Abednego came out of the fire, and the satraps, prefects, governors and royal advisers crowded around them. They saw that the fire had not harmed their bodies, nor was a hair of their heads singed; their robes were not scorched, and there was <u>no smell of fire on them</u>.*
>
> — **Daniel** 3:27 (emphasis added)

Isn't it amazing that there is no residue of their ordeal? They brought nothing out with them. This is how I have found this brother to be, and others who have exemplified forgiveness: no smell of smoke, but the aroma of Christ.

So is there a good way to go? Can leaving be done well? Before we started what was to become LifeLine Church, Dawn and I felt that we needed to leave the local Pentecostal church. There were lots of reasons: the greatest was that we felt that this church was not able to be a full expression of how church should be, according to what we were starting to understand at that time. At the start of the 'restoration' or house church movement, many of the different denominations were unable to contain this new revelation and expression of church: they couldn't and wouldn't adapt. We didn't know exactly what we should be going to, but knowing that the answer to the longing in us for a radical new expression of church was not to be found in – or allowed to grow up in – our home church, we had to leave. For a period of time we attended another meeting, which a friend of mine had invited us to. It's funny – we soon learned that we had exchanged one set of meetings for another: there was no more church life here. Their way of integrating us was just to invite us to more meetings; there was no real offer of fellowship and relationship, and we knew it would be a swift sojourn. The key was that once we knew we were going, we went: we didn't hang around, we didn't undermine what was there – we had a different vision, a different calling, and so we went. And that is the best way. Why be there once you have decided to go? Just go.

So why write about these painful experiences? Well, strange as it may seem, many of these trials have actually become 'monument stones' – the acts of God in our lives, things that we have come through, growing in the process. We are on a pilgrimage, always learning and seeking to find God's purpose in all circumstances, not settling in bitterness, or for what we are comfortable with.

We don't know the end that God has planned, and we would often prefer not to have to learn this way – but, as Paul says while carrying the thorn in his side, 'we know that in all things God works for the good of those who love him, who have been called according to his purpose' (Rom. 8:28). Not everything is finished: some 'leavings' we are still pained by; some we have come through; some we are in the midst of, and are praying for a Godly conclusion – but life is meant to be 'abundant' (John 10:10). That is, there is to be lots of it, and it should be rich rather than bland. We need the hard experiences, the shadow, to emphasise the light – the great things God has done, for which we are so grateful.

The 'Valley of Baka' is often translated as a valley of tears or weeping; so the location of the journey is no easy place, dry and barren – but the result of the pilgrims passing is dramatic: they make it a place of springs! Why is that? How can they have this effect? It's because of the state of their hearts, not their engineering skills.

The subject of this book, pilgrimage, could also be described as 'adventure'. All of us are called to tackle the places we are called to – be they work, home, school, college, university; or relationships with friends, neighbours, colleagues – with a spirit of adventure and a readiness to respond to the 'now' word of God.

The Spirit of Adventure

This chapter is a little risky. So far, all that we have shared is in the past and has been worked out and reflected on. However, from all we have said it would be wrong to look only backwards: we don't have a looking-back faith, and we don't want to have a looking-back nature. So this next part looks forward. We don't know how we will reflect in a number of years' time on what we write here, but we thought you could take the risk with us.

Pilgrimage – what's in a name?

> *Blessed are those whose strength is in you,*
> *whose hearts are set on pilgrimage.*
> *As they pass through the Valley of Baka,*
> *they make it a place of springs;*
> *the autumn rains also cover it with pools.*
> *They go from strength to strength,*
> *till each appears before God in Zion.*
>
> — Ps. 84:5–7

If there was ever a verse that describes our journey, in the prophetic and in experience, this is it. We have seen that God has been gracious to us since the start, and brought us a sense of direction through words, pictures and scriptures; these directions are the prophetic in operation for us. Always travelling, never settling – it sounds more tortuous than it has actually been, although certainly not all who started the journey have continued to journey with us. Some have been called to other things; sadly, some have settled for something less – but we seem to never stop.

If this calling were just about travelling, like a collective wandering, this would be a strange and somewhat futile process. However, the key word here is 'pilgrimage': this is not some purposeless ambling – it is the most purposeful action. This is the tireless pursuit of what God has laid out: His path, His promise and His destination. It's worth looking at some different interpretations of verse 5. Although the wording changes the emphasis comes through:

> *How blessed is the man whose strength is in You,*
> *In whose heart are the highways <u>to Zion</u>!*
>
> — Ps. 84:5, NASB

> *And how blessed all those in whom you live,*
> *whose lives become roads you travel*
>
> — Ps. 84:5, MSG

It is so easy to settle – to decide that we don't really want to obtain those high heights that require constant striving and effort to achieve. For those who have ascended Everest, the journey seems to be an almost impossible battle against one's own flesh and blood. The heights that God calls us to, similarly, can only be achieved by a relentless battle against the flesh. Why settle for second best? When we can be the road the Lord travels, our destination and our being are wrapped up in 'Zion' (I see Zion not as the physical destination of Jerusalem in the Middle East, but the ultimate destination of those who follow Jesus. It is the place He has for us, a place to strain towards, or the 'goal' that Paul speaks of). Gene Edwards captures something of this sense of high calling, in the dedication of his book *Climb the Highest Mountain* to the young men he worked with:

> *I trust that in that future hour, I will see you as I saw you… high up on a mountain… with a banner in your hand… and a gleam in your eye*[29]

In the book of Mehemiah, dedication to the mission and the vision is very much at the centre of Nehemiah's responses to Sanballat and co, who are constantly trying to hinder the work Nehemiah is about: rebuilding the walls of Jerusalem. In Nehemiah 6, they come calling with a seemingly innocent invitation to a meeting. Nehemiah spots

---

29 Edwards, G. (1984). *Climb the Highest Mountain* (formerly entitled *Our Mission*). Beaumont, TX: The SeedSowers.

this for what it is: a distraction and a desire to do him harm, and he responds appropriately: I am building a wall and I cannot come down! (Neh. 6:3)

So often we have had to turn to this story and have a similar determination to watch out for distractions or, to borrow from military terminology, attacks on the flank. As an army commander, you cannot ignore the flanking attack, but neither can you make it your whole focus if you are still to achieve your objectives. Distractive, flanking actions often come in the guise of fads or traditions – 'this is how we do things around here'-type statements, all wrapped up as well-meaning advice. That's why our hearts need to be set on pilgrimage: this isn't just a day out – it's a journey. How dangerous to view a trek through the jungle as a day at the park: the fact that you would forget to take the necessary equipment is an obvious issue, but the mindset is the key difference.

It all sounds a bit like hard work – a painful trudge. But of course, this is not the promise; 'As they pass through the Valley of Baka, they make it a place of springs.' The 'Valley of Baka' is often translated as a valley of tears or weeping; so the location of the journey is no easy place, dry and barren – but the result of the pilgrims passing is dramatic: they make it a place of springs! Why is that? How can they have this effect? It's because of the state of their hearts, not their engineering skills. They can have an expectation that they will positively change the world around them, the very society they are part of. Not only is their environment affected, but they are renewed and changed as well: 'They go from strength to strength, till each appears before God in Zion'. So our determination to be a people whose hearts are set on pilgrimage is not about some sort of penitent self-flagellation, or 'worm theology'; we wish to affect the valleys around us and, as we pass through, make them fruitful and no longer desolate – and we also have every expectation that we will go from strength to strength while we are at it!

Spirit of adventure

In some ways the pilgrimage can also be described as an adventure. We are not all about to jump out of a plane, or fight in a physical battle, but we can take the spirit of adventure to wherever we find ourselves: work, home, school, college; in our relationships with our neighbours, school friends or workmates; wherever we are.

Much of this relates to how we respond to the 'now word' of God – which of course means we need to appreciate that there is a 'now word': that what was good yesterday may not be what God has for us today. There is thus a need to travel from one place to another; to move from one paradigm to another. It's no good despising what came before, but equally it is no good resisting what God is bringing to us today. When the cloud moves we have to move with it; as the children of Israel also found, the good manna of yesterday could not be preserved; they needed to move on. We don't want a stale faith.

This journeying of the children of Israel from Egypt to the Promised Land is indeed the biblical image that best captures the idea of pilgrimage. There were many temptations to step aside from the journey, but they had to press on. There was a purification as they went, and a generation did not make it to the Promised Land; even Moses had only a sight of it, and didn't experience the new promise. So we could conclude that this is all about change and about shedding what we have learnt from the past like an old skin, were it not for this:

> *Moses took the <u>bones of Joseph</u> with him because Joseph had made the Israelites swear an oath. He had said, "God will surely come to your aid, and then you must carry my bones up with you from this place.*
>
> — **Ex. 13:19** (emphasis added)

There is a sense of the heritage that the Israelites took with them. So transition, pilgrimage and adventure does not mean forgetting all that we have learnt, despising what God has given us, missing out on the foundational values that have been set in us. Those things are mobile and can travel and even inform our next journey.[30]

---

30 In Joshua 24 we see that the Israelites bury Joseph's bones in land that they have retaken. This takes place just after Joshua dies, and it seem likely that this was one of his final requests – it was therefore very important to him.

Adventure sometimes means taking steps into a place that God has set for us without seeing any evidence that we will have influence or authority in that new situation. We assume a position given to us by God's promise, but we do so not by the evidence of our eyes. When God calls Gideon while he is hidden in the wine press, a picture of futile cowardice and self-preservation, Gideon is addressed: 'The LORD is with you, mighty warrior.' (Judg. 6:12–13) You might wonder how the angel managed to say this with a straight face, particularly when we hear Gideon's response: 'Pardon me...' Gideon has to take hold of the promise that God has called him to be a 'mighty warrior'; he does not stand on his own track record, but on this promise of his future identity. That's pretty risky – or better described as adventurous. Risk and hope add a freshness to our faith, and this is a good antidote to staleness.

It is a new thing to receive the call to stand out and be radical. We are familiar with Jesus' charge to be salt and light, but do we really consider what it means to be a 'city on a hilltop'? (Matt. 5:13) A city is not a passing thing, like a flavour or a torch; there is intentionality and corporateness to it. To be a city there must be building and planning, relationship and purpose. It makes me reflect on the story of Epaphroditus. He is sent by the church in Philippi to aid Paul, but when he arrives he becomes sick and almost dies. Far from being an aide, he is now a drain on Paul, and he would seem to be homesick in the midst of this – Paul is quite keen to send him home. But Paul is not dismissive of Epaphroditus. He says:

> *So then, welcome him in the Lord with great joy, and honour people like him, because he almost died for the work of Christ. He <u>risked his life</u> to make up for the help you yourselves could not give me.*
>
> — **PHIL. 2:29–30** (emphasis added)

Epaphroditus risked his life, and failed! Yet Paul says to honour him. That's risk and the freshness of faith: nothing conservative or stale here – and not all adventures go the way we expect.

We see a great adventurer in Caleb. He can sometimes be overshadowed by Joshua, but his story is still significant. Caleb is sent as one of the twelve spies into Canaan; the result was that ten wanted to turn back. Caleb says, 'We should go up and take possession of the land, for we can certainly do it' (Num. 13:30). They had all seen the same things: there was no doubt that there was both fruitfulness and giants in the land. However, what was telling was not how the others saw the land and the occupants of the land, but how they saw themselves. Whereas Caleb says 'we can certainly do it' with a sense of expectant risk, this is set against the ten who say 'We seemed like grasshoppers in our own eyes...' (Num. 13:33). The desire of Caleb and Joshua was to save the people, despite the people's negative talk throughout the night: 'And do not be afraid of the people of the land, because we will devour them. Their protection is gone, but the Lord is with us. Do not be afraid of them.' (Num. 14:9). But it is no use – Caleb and Joshua are at risk of being stoned by the people.

It is important to notice that Caleb's spirit of adventure does not dissipate: neither his reception by the children of Israel, nor the forty years that pass before he enters the land, change his commitment. His 'wholeheartedness' is noted by Joshua (Josh. 14) – the Message version describes how Caleb 'stuck to his guns'! Forty years later, as he asks for the land Moses promised him, that land still needs to be cleared of the race of giants who occupy it!

> *...and now behold, I am eighty-five years old today. I am still as strong today as I was in the day Moses sent me...*
> — JOSH. 14:10–11, NASB

Would it not be great to carry that same energy and passion at 85? Not only this, but we see that he has bred this cheeky, demanding nature into those around him: his adventurous spirit is seen in his daughter Aksah. She is given in marriage to a warrior who takes key territory for Caleb, but she urges her husband to go further and ask for a field, and then she asks Caleb to give her another wedding gift of land with springs. Caleb sees some of himself in her and gives her this. He has bred those who will not settle for less, as he did not settle for less (Judg. 1). That's a great picture for us: are we restless for the promises God has for us? And do we grow that restlessness in those around us – our families, extended families or spheres of influence? Like Joshua and Caleb our intention is that all cross into the Promised Land – all of our people and all of our children.

Possessing the Gate

In the book of Esther, we see how Esther also finds herself in the midst of an adventure. I think that by now we can recognise that adventures are not always enjoyable at every stage – certainly her life is at risk, as well as the lives of those around her. The spirit of adventure is about *how* we embrace the opportunity to be about God's work, as well as the adventure itself. Esther finds herself with an outside chance of speaking up for her people; if it doesn't work, they will die and she is very likely to join them. This is a kind of political drama: one of influencing and forming policy.

We see that Mordecai, Esther's uncle, is to be found sitting at the gate (Est. 2:19). This location is key: it is at the gate where policy is decided. This is the place to be if you want to know or influence what is going on – it is the place for the movers and shakers. It is here that Mordecai hears of a plot to kill the king. He is again found at the gate when the plot turns against him and the Jews. He is in this place of influence; he is in touch with the times and seasons in the political world around him, and he is there to support Esther in her role. Mordecai challenges Esther: 'And who knows but that you have come to royal position <u>for such a time as this?</u>' (Est. 4:14; emphasis added). She does not take this lightly, but asks for some 'prayer cover' and goes to the king.

Influencing systems and impacting individuals have been the underlying aims and flavour of our work in the community through LifeLine Projects. However, our desire as a community to positively affect those around us, and to bring a solution-focused challenge to the systems and policy we come across, is not just restricted to LifeLine Projects but really goes through all of LifeLine like the letters in a stick of rock.

We have recognised that God has been calling us to be 'possessors of the gate', to stand in this space. The whole idea of possessing the gate is about having significant influence. Of course we all have the opportunity to be witnesses of Christ wherever we are. We shine a light. But possessing the gate speaks of being in a place where justice is dispensed, policy decided. This is the role that Joseph and Daniel had, as well as Esther: not being the king or policy maker, but having influence in those arenas.

As was the case for Esther, to understand the possibilities and the position in which we find ourselves, but also to be aware of God's timing. 'We have to know God's mind and His moment!'

We are now choosing to recognise the placing of God. I will not go through all the areas of significance in which we find ourselves, but we see that much of what has been planted in us in the past has relevance today, in ways the potency of which we have never seen before. This is the case both in the UK and abroad, and both within the church and – indeed, mostly – outside of the confines of what is known as church. What we want to do is recognise more swiftly where these God-placements are occurring, so that we can send out individuals just as we do when we as an apostolic community send people on trips abroad: we want to pray for and support those who are being sent to areas of influence.

Extending reach – the lead follower

If we are to embrace as a community the fact that there will be some possessing/speaking/standing at the gates, and we see this as part of our collective calling, it stands to reason that there is a part for all to play. This is not about equality of roles: we are not all the same – we don't all get the same badge – but we all share in the sending and the supporting.

A number of years ago when I was travelling a lot and the boys were younger and at home with Dawn, we noticed over a number of trips that there were several big issues that hit while I was away. Some building work went very wrong and the builders had to start again; Jamie was bitten across the face by a dog; the house was burgled; and Daniel was beaten up on the way home from school. We realised that sending and supporting had to take on a new role. A team of intercessors formed to pray for my trip and ministry, but just as important was that there would also be prayer and support for the family at home.

We want now to do the same again for this new season of placement and influence with God, as more of us become 'sent ones' or 'apostles' to other areas of influence: education, health, politics, music, community development and so on. We as a people want to give support and prayer, in recognition of God's sending and strategy.

As Derek Siver says in a TED talk on '*How to start a movement*',[31] the first follower changes a 'lone nut' into a leader. In western, individualistic society we have been sold a restrictive narrative: either you are a leader with a vision or you are second best. The result of this is that there are some who are made to be the shoulders, the hands and feet, who are always striving to be the head – both within the church and outside. We have been told if you are not leading, you are not achieving your potential – you are somehow a let-down, you have given up on your destiny. But surely, it is more important to be a part than the part you play.

Yet we know that no visionary can operate on their own: yes, they need followers, but they need *supporters* – people who get things done. In my early Christian life, I was very much the support act. I had a car so I served by driving, and I was able to connect with people on the street – drug addicts and so on – so I would bring them to Len Halls, who would then minster to them in his home. Some of those who were part of the Pentecostal church where Len and I were would say, 'John, this is your ministry, not Len's!' They were trying to butter me up, but I was very happy with the role I had – we recognised each other's part: he was the senior minister, but we were in this together and there was no striving for position. As time went on and I left that church, Len's son David became the leader of the group we were in and I served under him. In due course I became the senior leader of the church, and now both Len and David were part of the leadership team: the roles had changed, but there was no despising what had gone on before.

These two roles of leader and supporter are not mutually exclusive: often we can be taking a lead in one area, but be rooting for those who are out in front in another.

Those who stand with the leader give impetus to what is happening. Daniel played rugby as a second row forward. He says he didn't do much, other than push in the scrums, rucks and mauls and jump at the line-out. He rarely got to carry the ball, and never to score a try – and there were not many tackles to be made either. However, as the second

---

31 Sivers, D. (2010). 'How to start a movement'. TED talk. Available at: www.ted.com/talks/derek_sivers_how_to_start_a_movement

row is the powerhouse and energy behind the direction of the team, without the power and drive they supply you can be pointing in the right direction and have a vision, but you won't get far.

In this way those who are the 'first followers' extend the reach of the group. Their 'following' can be through prayer and practical support, through questioning or being a sounding board; sometimes it's just through being a friend and having fun. Of course, sometimes there are related assignments, research or tasks, all vitally important. The glorious parts of military campaigning are tactics and strategy, but logistics are of equal importance: Napoleon said 'An army marches on its stomach,' whereas Churchill spoke of the battle for the Atlantic, against the U-boats disrupting the food supplies and aid sailing to Britain during the second world war, as 'The only thing that ever really frightened me'.[32]

Characters worth examination

There are many Bible characters who played this kind of supporting role, extending the reach of others. We saw the faithful and untiring nature of Caleb, and we have seen the significant part that Mordecai played in the trajectory of Esther's life. Mordecai seems to have been a constant prompting to Esther; he nurtured her to begin with, and took her into his own home – she was like a daughter to him. Fathering those who are not our own children is so important, just as Mordecai does for Esther; there is plenty of opportunity for this. Remember these opportunities come when we are tired, and have other pressures – they don't wait for our feelings to be ready. Mordecai is under threat when he is giving this input to Esther; he could have seen her concerns as trivial, whereas he was in the midst of trying just to survive. Mordecai also has a role in bringing out Esther's best: in some ways we can say he was midwife to her anointing. So there is a pattern for us to see here involving those who support and nurture. They may not give their name to the title of a book (Esther has Mordecai; Joshua has Caleb), but they are vital.

---

32 Churchill, W. (1949). *The Second World War, Volume II: Their Finest Hour* (2005 edition). London: Penguin.

Jonathan has another such supporting role. Everyone around him would have expected him to be the next king, but he sees, and aligns himself with a vision for David which works against his own inheritance. Recognising God's anointing on another is what Jonathan shows us. He looks beyond the natural order of things and is willing to play a subordinate role. He also has a part to play in encouragement and cajoling.

Then there are the stories of promotion and demotion that Elisha and Barnabus demonstrate. Elisha serves Elijah and requests a double portion of his anointing. Barnabus takes Saul/Paul with him on his missionary trip, and soon Paul becomes the leading figure.

There is something humbling about the story of John the Baptist, who could be seen merely as the 'warm-up act' for Jesus. But the Bible does not put it like this – he was there to 'prepare the way' (Mark 1:3). This phrase describes one of the crucial roles of the lead follower: that sense of preparing the ground. A building cannot be built, and a field cannot be planted or harvested, without the preparation of the ground. Often unseen and certainly unrecognised, groundworks are expensive and there can be little to show for the investment, but without them the vision does not take hold. How often have you come across a disgruntled homeowner who is having an extension built on to their house? All they can see to start with is a large trench in their back garden. 'It feels I'm pouring money into the ground,' they say, yet just see what happens if those foundations are not there – the building can never be established.

I have seen the dangers of an 'ideas person' or visionary without those around who will make the thing happen. There has to be some submission by the visionary to those who are given to help realise the vision. Sometimes, in biblical terms, this person is called the 'helmsman'[33]: he who gives a steer to achieve the path or route that the ship's master or captain determines. Without the helmsman directing resources and holding to the route, the ship will not go anywhere.

---

33 The Greek word for administration in 1 Cor. 12:28, *Kuberneses*, literally means the pilot or helmsman of a ship. The notable things about pilots are: they follow or guide in a direction; they take instructions from the captain; they have responsibility; and the ship is not their own, but entrusted to them for the task.

Lois and Eunice, grandmother and mother of Timothy, and Hannah, mother of Samuel, show another aspect of being in the supporting role: that of being active influencers. Lois and Eunice have nurtured a character in Timothy ready for his calling with Paul. They surely have some claim to have influenced the person of whom Paul would say, 'I have no one else like Timothy, who genuinely cares about your welfare' (Phil. 2:20, NLT). Paul himself gives credit to this planting by Lois and Eunice in his second letter to Timothy. Hannah shows a similar pattern in nurturing Samuel while not holding on to him: taking the child she has invested in, holding him lightly and handing him over to God's service – still not losing interest, but maintaining an involvement.

The normal radical, or church as a polo?

Much of this book is shaped by our desire not to lose what God has taught us, and to share with those who wish to learn from our journey. As we have looked at these good building blocks in LifeLine Church in London, in recent times, we have said that the values God gave us in the past are still solid and good – we just need to determine the shape of the building we are to make out of them. We want to return to our roots, to the meaning of 'radical', and we want it to be our normal position to be radical and in touch with our God-given values – hence the idea of the 'normal radical'. We do not want to prescribe a way of being, but to take the core building bricks, reclaim them, knock off the mortar – the constructs, styles and interpretations of the past – and rebuild for the future. We believe the 'bricks' are still good: the values and learning – the 'bones of Joseph' – need to travel with us, but we don't know the final shape of what we are building. In fact, it would be dangerous to say we have arrived, to set up a structure and say we have all revealed truth. We always want to be focused on why we do things, not just what we do. We know there is more to come, and that's why we have to have our hearts set on pilgrimage.

On the other hand, if we don't take those values with us, those life lessons, we lose our centre. Far from being a 'church as a force', we are a 'church as a polo': we are centreless, involved in activity without quite knowing why, other than the fact that it feels familiar.

Sherpa general store

We see ourselves as being like the last store before the great mountain ascent. It's a good place to get equipped – plus we have an added advantage: we have been here before, we know how to proceed! So we will equip our fellow travellers and be guides, like Sherpas – we want you to succeed, to obtain new heights.

> *[Jesus] said, "Then you see how every student well-trained in God's kingdom is like the owner of a <u>general store</u> who can put his hands on anything you need, old or new, exactly when you need it."*
> — **Matt. 13:52 MSG** (emphasis added)

This is the season for us: we are poised to equip others. Of course, we are still seeking new heights ourselves. We don't want to miss out – after all,

> *'Blessed are those... whose hearts are set on pilgrimage'.*

Also from LifeLine and FaithAction

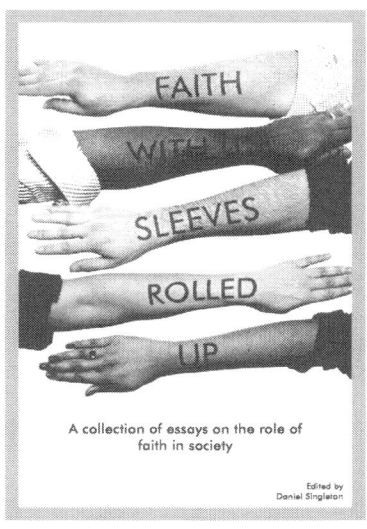

How To Guides – Event Planning, Social Enterprise and more
Building Dementia-Friendly Faith Communities
Keeping Pressure Off Hospitals
Making the Case for Faith and Health
Faith and Domestic Abuse: Recommendations for Faith Leaders
What a Difference Faith Makes to… Homelessness
What a Difference Faith makes to… Alcohol Abuse

Resources for charities and faith groups available from FaithAction
www.faithaction.net

Find out more about LifeLine at

LifeLine Church
www.lifelinechurch.co.uk

LifeLine Projects
www.lifelineprojects.co.uk

LifeLine Network
www.lifelinenetwork.org.uk

Community Resources
www.communityresources.co.uk

Printed in Great Britain
by Amazon